Foreword

When I met Selma Cook, she had just started working on the book *'Buried Treasure'*. At first, I thought it was a book based on hunting for treasure. However, to my surprise, when I read it, I discovered that the 'treasure' is in fact spiritual treasure, not material treasure.

The Amirah Stevenson series is about the journey, and often humorous adventures, of a small Muslim family from Australia. Amirah is on the threshold of adolescence, and faced with life's complexities has only her father and spritely grandmother to turn to for advice.

This wonderful series is especially pertinent to Muslim teenagers who are thrown off balance by the many challenges in today's world. It is foremost for adolescents who are searching for meaning and understanding, and who struggle to maintain a balance between such influences and their commitment to their very special religion.

Naseema Mall

Journalist, South Africa

Dedication

To my children and my children's children, whose dreams awaken me and whose smiles lift my heart.

Amirah Stevenson Series

Part Two

The Colour of Fear

By Selma Cook

All rights reserved.

Copyright © 2023 Selma Cook

No part of this book may be used, distributed, or reproduced by any means, including photocopying, recording, taping, or by any other electronic, graphic, or mechanical methods without the written permission of the author, except in the case of brief quotations embodied in critical reviews and other noncommercial use permitted by copyright laws.

Many of the events and situations in this book were experienced by either the author herself or people who are close to the author. To protect the privacy of certain individuals, the names and identifying details have been changed.

Author: Selma Cook

ISBN 978-0-6458463-3-1 (Paperback)

ISBN 978-0-6458463-4-8 (E-book)

A Catalog record for this book is available from the National Library of Australia

CHAPTER 1

Up! Up! and Away

The rows and rows of blue chairs in the departure lounge were filled with people. Despite the large crowd there was not much noise. Amirah sat gazing at the people around her. Everyone was absorbed in something. One man opened a newspaper and buried himself within its folded edges. A tired woman sat a squirming child on her knee and tried in every conceivable way to prevent him from crying. A lonely old man with a small, old-fashioned black hat sat tidily on a chair with a bag in his lap, minding his own business. He caught Amirah's eye and smiled. Amirah smiled back.

Amirah had been rolling her boarding pass around and around her index finger for so long it looked as if it would need a warm iron to return it to its original shape. She leaned back on her blue chair with her feet crossed at the ankles. She was calm and comfortable except for the incessant rolling and twirling.

"Hey Amirah!" said Adam quietly in half a whisper. "Catch!"

He sat just a short distance in front of her. The blue of his shirt matched the blue of his eyes. He stretched out his legs to nudge her foot with his.

A small, soft, brightly colored ball plopped into her lap. A broad smile lit up her face.

"Not here, Dad. Everyone will think we're crazy."

"They might already," he answered wryly. "Let's not disappoint anyone."

Amirah rolled her eyes. When her dad had that look on his face there was no stopping him. They were going to play catch in the airport lounge where they waited, along with a few hundred other people, to board the plane to Egypt.

"What do you think Granny?" asked Amirah, as Granny sat comfortably, looking out of the huge windows at the tarmac beneath. She was watching a gigantic jumbo jet taxiing into position, being prepared to carry them off to their destination. Granny's soft hands were folded in her lap and her head tilted slightly to the side as she watched, waited, and thought.

"Think about what dear?" she finally answered.

"Dad wants to play catch and I think everyone is looking."

"There's only a small distance between you. I don't think you'll bother anyone." She scanned the blank faces surrounding her.

"And it's not breaking any rules and they can play too if they like."
Granny smiled warmly and Amirah saw the familiar happy lines around her old green eyes.

"So, Princess. You ready?" asked Adam. He leaned forward and wiped his hand over his curly hair. He had a distinctly mischievous look on his face and his eyes twinkled merrily as he pretended to aim the ball at Amirah's nose.

"Why?" asked Amirah. "I'm not good at this!"

"Well, we have to do something to save your boarding pass from being ripped to shreds. If you keep winding it up like that, they'll have to spin you around to unravel it!" declared her dad.

"Go on Amirah. Give it a try. Just concentrate," coaxed Granny.

Amirah had to unwind the boarding pass from her finger and hand it to Granny before she could settle herself on the chair and raise her hands into a catching position in front of her.

"Try to catch it with two fingers!" reminded Granny.

"Say when you're going to toss it over Dad."

"When!" he said, and the colorful ball flitted like a rounded clumsy butterfly and collided with Amirah's unsteady fingers and fell softly to the floor.

"You're not concentrating Princess," said Adam, as he scooped up the ball and prepared himself for another throw. He was determined.

"Listen dear, just clear your mind of all your worries. Don't think about what's around you. Focus on the ball," said Granny, with a descriptive wave of her hands.

When Granny and Adam played 'Catch' she rarely missed, and Adam seemed to have some kind of radar. He hardly missed anything at all.

Amirah's face went blank. She focused her eyes and relaxed her muscles. She could do this better at home on comfy cushions, tossing the ball back and forward to Dad but, here, in the airport on the way to a new country, a new everything – she wasn't so sure.

"Come on. Trust yourself," said Adam.
Her dad's words echoed in her mind. She started to think about home, The Retreat, the sea, her friends, walking to school, the rain, the blue sky.... "Got it!" she cried.

Amirah sat upright and stared at the ball in her hands.

"That's my girl," said Adam, before tweaking her nose, and tugging her off the chair. "Time to go," he said aloud with a cheery smile.
He scooped up all the bags and flung them comfortably over his shoulder and Amirah had to break into a half run to keep up with his long strides.

Granny gathered her papers and hurried to take Amirah's hand. She gave it a little squeeze.

"Come on then love. There's nothing like an adventure! And Australia is making it easy to say goodbye with this low grey sky and freezing cold wind." Amirah turned and stared out of the huge windows in the waiting lounge, but she didn't have time to think about anything as she was whisked out and onto the plane. She tried to ignore the butterflies in her stomach. She clutched the soft colorful ball, but no matter how she tried, she couldn't wind it around her finger.

CHAPTER 2

Time for Take off?

Once safely on the plane, Amirah snuggled down in her seat between Granny on the window seat and Adam on the aisle. The people on the plane were busy organizing bags, overhead lockers, and seating arrangements. Granny had her handbag planted firmly on her knee. This bag went with Granny wherever she went. It was a black shoulder bag faded to a soft supple leather that wrinkled at the edges. It looked as if it had traveled the world as indeed it had.

Adam was busy trying to arrange his seating posture and was forever saying, "Excuse me" or "sorry" when his feet got in the way of someone passing down the aisle. The flight attendant smiled and asked if they were comfortable and if they needed anything. After a short while everyone was miraculously seated in their places, bags were stowed away, and the plane was revving up for take-off.

"*Bismillah*," said Granny quietly as she snuggled down into her seat.

"It will be a long flight dear," said Granny to Amirah.

"I know," said Amirah excitedly. "This is my first time on a plane!"

From where she was sitting, she could see through the window.

"You don't mind me sitting next to the window do you, dear?" asked Granny.

"Not at all Granny. I don't want you to feel bad on the plane and if sitting there helps you, then go right ahead."

"Yes, I don't feel so good sometimes once they close the door," said Granny, pointing to the nearby door of the plane.

Sure enough, it wasn't long before the flight attendant closed and sealed the door. Granny winced a little when she heard the snap of the lock.

"Why do you feel like that Granny?" asked Amirah, looking up at her.

"Don't know exactly, dear. I just have an uncomfortable feeling whenever I'm in small, confined places."

"Don't worry Mum, just look out of the window and you'll see all the open space you need," commented Adam with a twinkle in his eye, "unless of course you're afraid of heights too!"

"Don't be cheeky young man. If I was afraid of heights as well, I would be traveling by ship!"

Amirah looked at Granny and then at her dad sitting next to her. A comfortable feeling rose in her heart, and she closed her eyes and stretched out. All she felt was a tremendous sense of excitement, a desire to see the world and be with the two people she loved most.

"By the way Adam dear, where do you propose to

put your legs during these long hours," asked Granny, teasing him back.

"Well, I thought I might fold them neatly around my neck, so no one trips over them."
Amirah laughed.

"You don't have to worry Dad. You can stretch them out into the aisle," suggested Amirah.

"You'll have half the plane stepping over your feet to get to the bathroom," commented Granny.

"I'll try not to bother anyone."

"Don't fall asleep Dad. The flight attendant has to bring the food and she'll never be able to push that cart past your feet."

"Just wake me up if I *nod off* Princess."
With that Adam stretched out his legs, put on his seat belt, pulled his small hat over his eyes, and went to sleep. In a few seconds he was breathing softly.

"How does Dad do that?" asked Amirah curiously.

Granny glanced over at him.

"I've never seen anyone who can sleep *at the drop of a hat* like your father, dear. Except of course your grandfather."

The Colour of Fear

Adam was six feet three inches tall with a broad but slim build. Summer or winter you would see him wearing his comfy trainers, blue jeans, and long shirt. On cold days like today, he wore his sheepskin jacket. His blonde curly hair and ginger beard framed a face that spoke of gentleness and kindness. Such softness belied the fact that he was famous for his skills in self-defense, especially karate. He was a quiet man who preferred to keep to himself and to observe the people and events that surrounded him. So, it is not surprising that he worked as a freelance journalist; and it was his expertise in this area that had led him to accept a job in Egypt with a company that wanted to make use of his writing talents.

Amirah rested her head on her father's shoulder and waited for the plane to take off.

"Granny."

"Yes dear."

"Why is Dad sleeping when the plane is going to take off any minute," she asked, as she felt it starting to move.

Granny smiled.

"Well dear, he doesn't like heights, just like I don't like enclosed places. So, he says it's better to sleep and not think about it."

"Good idea," said Amirah. "But if he is so afraid of heights he should have gone by boat."

"That's not your dad. He tries to confront his fears."

"Well, he's not confronting them by sleeping, is he Granny?"

"He's halfway there."

Amirah looked at her dad sleeping peacefully, and she sighed, thinking how little she knew about him. At fourteen years of age, she had only just begun to realize how much she didn't know about people, even those who were closest to her.

"Why didn't Dad ever say anything about that?" asked Amirah.

"I suppose it's one of the battles he fights within himself. You'll find dear, that people are generally afraid of something."

"I don't think I'm afraid of anything," said Amirah, thinking out loud.
Granny smiled at her lovingly.

"I hope you stay like that, but even if one day you find you are afraid of something, just remember that only

Allah can help us *and* make our hearts strong."

The plane was now moving rapidly down the runway and Amirah's eyes opened wide with excitement. She turned to her dad and almost woke him up, but then remembered that it was better to let him sleep until they were already in the air. Granny was staring out the window, focusing on something. Amirah was gazing around at the people and enjoying the feeling of moving up into the air, leaving behind the land that she had always moved on. Her ears started to pop, and she put some chewing gum into her mouth and started chewing madly. Soon the popping in her ears eased and when she looked again the city was so far below and fluffy clouds bounced around outside the window.

She glanced at her dad and smiled, thinking of how he was sleeping through his fear and then she looked again at Granny who sat, staring at one picture in the magazine that lay on her lap.

"People don't seem to talk when they're facing fear," thought Amirah. So, with no one to talk to, she snuggled down between the two people she loved most in the world. She felt safe.

CHAPTER 3

Passing Time

"I'm bored," moaned Amirah. "We've only just got out of Australia!" She was studying the map on the screen in front of them.

"Yes dear, it takes about six hours to get out of Australia. That's quite remarkable, isn't it?" observed Granny.

"Well, Princess, we still have quite a few hours to go until we arrive in Bangkok for a stopover, then you can get out and stretch your legs, *inshaa Allah*," said Adam, trying to stop yawning.

"I've seen so much of Australia today from up here and, *Masha Allah*, I never knew that most of the ground in central Australia is red," commented Amirah. "How beautiful it is! Really amazing. I don't think I'll ever forget it," she said wistfully.

"We're going to the land of golden sand Princess," said Adam. "There is beauty in every place on earth, don't worry. *Insha Allah* you have many more beautiful things to see in your life."

"I can't see anything right now except white clouds dear," said Granny, looking out the window but later you'll see the blueness of the ocean."

"That's when I hope I'm sound asleep," commented Adam, shifting in his seat as he prepared to nap once again.

"Granny, you know Dad's real boring in planes. I never knew that about him before," commented Amirah in a loud whisper, winking at Granny.

"I heard that," said Adam from under sleepy eyes. "Maybe it's time for the buzzing bee."

"No! No! Dad! Not on the plane."

Adam started to make a soft buzzing noise and moved his hand like a bee searching for a target. It headed straight for Amirah's shoulder.

"Dad! If I scream the people will think ....!" Amirah looked daring.

"Go ahead. You can scream. I'll just explain to everyone what a tiresome little........buzzzz, Gotcha!"

"OOOw!" said Amirah playfully, with a stifled cry. "Hey Dad! Only one sting you know! Bees don't sting more than once! Dad!"

Adam's 'bee' buzzed around some more and this time landed on Amirah's nose.

"Oh! This isn't a sting, it's a pinch," said Adam laughing now, as he tweaked her nose and then the 'bee' rested on the tray table in front of Amirah.

"You're a cheeky bee," said Amirah, and tried to shoo it away with a magazine.

"Come on you two, you're disturbing my concentration. I'm trying to think peaceful, happy thoughts," smiled Granny. "Can't you have some mercy for an old woman with claustrophobia," said Granny, quietly making a hissing noise like someone with no teeth.

Amirah knew very well that Granny still had all her teeth. She laughed aloud.

"Mum, you're not old. Sorry, no sympathy for age," commented Adam, teasing.

"Yes. Okay but I am your mother, no matter how old you may be!" said Granny, asserting herself. "And," she added, "mothers are to be respected and, well, listened to and…"

"Yes Mum, you're the queen and little red nose over here is the princess."

"So, what does that make you Dad?" asked Amirah with a cheeky smile.

"I'm the *mahram*," said Adam grandly with a pleased look on his sleepy, but comical face. "By the way ladies, just remember that without me, your *mahrum*, you wouldn't be traveling like you are right now. I expect some appropriate respect and good behavior from you both," added Adam, who half closed his eyes to appear prouder of himself.

"This time he's gone too far," said Granny, laughing. "Wish I had the water spray bottle," she said quietly, "that would bring him quickly to himself again," she snickered, thinking of the pleasure of wiping that idiotic smirk off his face.

"No Granny," said Amirah winking at her, "Dad's right. We must respect him as he deserves."

"And respect him we do," added Granny wryly.

"He's our *mahram* and really Granny, he's one in a million, you know. I really don't know what I'd do without him."

"Yes dear, such a treasure," added Granny, settling down for a good tease.

Adam was stretched out and half asleep, but he could hear the teasing in their voices and kept his eyes shut hoping they would continue.

"Yes Granny. This dad of mine, works for us!"

"Pays for us," added Granny.

"Worries about how he will pay my bills," said Amirah reflectively.

"Carries the shopping for us," remarked Granny.

"Opens the door for us."

"Protects us!"

"Makes great spaghetti sauce! And cleans the kitchen better than me," said Amirah.

"That wouldn't be hard dear," commented Granny.

"He reads me bedtime stories," said Amirah, ignoring Granny's comment.

"Fixes my car!"

"Helps me with my homework."

"Takes me to visit my friends," added Granny.

"I could just go on and on," stated Amirah, with a wave of her hands.

"Okay you two," said Adam, getting the drift. "Who said that Muslim women were oppressed?"

"Not us!" Granny and Amirah said in unison. Quiet laughter filled the air.

"Now if you don't mind," said Adam with an elaborate expression of fake ill humor, "I think I'll have *forty winks*, that is, if you don't have any doors to open, bills to pay, shopping to carry, dinner to cook, kitchens to clean or cars to fix…"

Adam didn't wait for an answer. He settled down again to forget where he was: 30,000 feet in the air, in a plane that bounced in clouds, hovering over the expansive ocean. No, no, it was time to sleep, not think.

Hours passed. The plane was fast approaching Bangkok airport.

CHAPTER 4

Bangkok Airport

A sharp jolt aroused the three from their dreams. Granny's sharp eyes were instantly alert. Adam half opened one eye and looked out the window. Amirah yawned and stretched, and asked, "What's going on?"

Before anyone could answer, a voice came over the loudspeaker, "Ladies and gentlemen, we are now approaching Bangkok airport. We are experiencing some turbulence. Could you please return to your seats and fasten your seat belts….."

The voice droned on a little more and smiling flight attendants walked around the aisles making sure seat belts were fastened.

Granny peered carefully out the window. It was pitch black and sheets of rain fell, making it impossible to see anything. Adam reached over to look out of the window. His knitted eyebrows were the only sign of concern, but Amirah saw his face and felt worried.

"What's going on Dad? Everyone is quiet." The murmuring of voices, occasional bursts of laughter, and chattering of people who were busy passing their time had become suddenly quiet.

"It's just a bit of a bumpy ride Princess. *Insha Allah* we'll land in a little while."

He settled back in his seat again, trying to ignore the heavy rocking of the plane.

"Granny, why is the plane moving like that? It feels strange."

Amirah was worried and her face was white. She had a sick feeling in her stomach. She reached toward the window, trying to see anything out there.

They all felt the plane going down and the engines roared very loudly. This wasn't the usual landing one might see in the movies. The air was filled with tension and the plane rocked from side to side, quite violently at times. Granny sat still, moving her lips quietly, making *du'aa* that they would land safely. Adam sat staring at the window, his mind filled with the words of the Qu'ran.

Amirah kept saying over and over, *"La hawla wa la quwatta illa billah."*

The plane roared, going lower and lower until Amirah thought surely the wheels should be touching the ground, then strangely, it started to move upwards again, still rocking from side to side.

"Dad!" demanded Amirah, 'What's going on?" Again, before he could answer, the same voice was on the loudspeaker, "Ladies and Gentlemen, we are experiencing some difficulty landing in Bangkok airport due to bad weather, but we will attempt landing again in a few minutes. Please do not remove your seat belts."

There were a few voices to be heard on the plane. From time to time a nervous laugh could be heard as flight attendants continued their walk, checking everything before taking their seats.

Again, the plane rocked from side to side and

lurched and bumped in the air like it was being thrown around by a giant hand. Once again, its engines roared and approached the ground only to soar back into the air once more.

Granny peered out the window, straining her eyes. She could see absolutely nothing through the blackness and rain, and she wondered if the pilot could. She hoped and prayed that he did.

It was some minutes before the pilot was heard again but this time, Adam detected a distinct quiver in his voice.

"Ladies and Gentlemen. The weather is extremely bad. Please prepare for a crash landing. The flight attendants will show you the brace position and there are life jackets under your seats."

Crash landing! Again, there was not a single sound to be heard from any of the passengers. Amirah stared at the people around her in the plane. They were all unfamiliar faces. No one was looking at anyone else. Everyone seemed to be concentrating on one spot, their eyes dazed. There was silent terror in many eyes.

"Are we going to crash?" asked Amirah, looking frantically from her Granny to her dad.

"*Inshaa Allah* not, dear," said Granny calmly. "Keep making *du'aa* and trust in Allah. Think positively."

Amirah stared at the seat in front of her and could think of nothing except *du'aa*. Her heart was filled with a giant void; a feeling that she could fall into it and keep falling and falling. She was afraid.

The rest of the passengers were leaning forward in their seats as requested by the captain, but Granny peered out of the window, straining her eyes once again to see any sign of light on the runway. Then as the plane lurched and rocked its way toward the ground, she saw lines of men with lanterns in their hands waving back and forward, forming lines to guide the plane safely onto the runway.

"*Alhumdulillah*," said Granny out loud.

Amirah had her head down for a while but couldn't resist the temptation to look up at what was going on around her. Feeling a little more composed, she looked around the plane but couldn't see a single person or hear one sound.

"Fear is silent," she thought to herself.

When she remembered Allah, she felt peace. The

feeling of fear didn't go away altogether but she felt a sense of comfort. After all, she knew that everyone has their time to leave this world, but like all people, she hoped it wouldn't be today. Not today.

The plane landed violently. There was a screeching noise that was almost unbearable, and Amirah covered her ears. The plane swerved from side to side and by the time it was brought under control it was almost facing the opposite direction.

At last, the engines died down and the realization that they had landed safely dawned on the passengers. Even the flight attendants started to smile again, but their faces seemed strained. Now that the danger had passed, it was surprising to Amirah how quickly the people had begun to laugh and joke again. Her hands were shaking as she reached for her bag. They had two hours before they had to board the same plane again.

CHAPTER 5

Recalled to Life

"Is the plane broken, Dad?" asked Amirah nervously.

"What makes you ask that Princess?" Adam was seated once again beside Amirah on the plane and getting ready for the final stage of their journey.

"Well, it made so much noise landing before. Maybe it blew out a tire or something."

"Don't worry, *Insha Allah*. Have you made the *du'aa* for traveling?" asked Adam.

"Yes of course. The same as I did when we got on the plane in Australia," said Amirah.

"Then don't worry. What's the point of making *du'aa* then worrying? There are technicians who check the plane when it lands and make sure it's ready for takeoff again."

"Your dad's right Amirah," said Granny. "This is a good lesson for all of us, you know. Everything is in the control of Allah, and it is our job to do the right things – make the right choices - and trust in Him. Come on, cheer up Princess."

Granny gave Amirah a sideways hug and showed her some pictures in the magazine.

Before they knew it, the plane was soaring in the air. Adam was fast asleep. Everything seemed normal.

"You know Granny," said Amirah after a while, "that crash landing thing really scared me."

"Me too dear. I must say, I wasn't expecting that."

"Life isn't very safe is it, Granny?"

"That's why we make *du'aa* all the time. It means we seek Allah's protection and guidance every footstep we take."

Adam sat up and stifled a yawn.

"Like before Princess," said Adam, "we were all startled and afraid but what did you do?"

"I asked Allah," said Amirah with wide eyes.

"Exactly," said Granny. "That's exactly what you should do."

"Question is," said Adam, "how did you feel?"

"I felt afraid at first but then I felt a bit peaceful, kind of like resigned to whatever happens," Amirah remembered.

"Now that feeling of peace, Princess," said Adam, "is a gift from Allah because you trust in Him."

"It's priceless dear," added Granny. "Having faith, doesn't mean you'll never feel fear, but it means you'll have the ability to cope with it and move forward despite it."

"Fear isn't necessarily a bad thing," added Adam. "Without it we wouldn't know danger, and sometimes Allah gives us a taste of it, so we can appreciate that wonderful feeling of peace even more."

Amirah listened in silence. This was a big subject, something she was thinking deeply about. Sometimes she found it difficult to express exactly what she wanted to say but this time, simply the expression on her face let her dad and Granny know that she was beginning to understand things that had often left her feeling confused before.

"Granny," said Amirah in a whisper, "I'm so glad I'm still alive."

Granny smiled at her and nodded.

"When we got onto the plane in Australia," whispered Amirah, snuggling up to Granny, "all we were thinking about was going to Egypt. Now all we are thinking about is the fact that we are still alive. It has only been a few hours; less than a day."

Granny gave her a hug and patted her hand.

"You're a good girl Amirah, *Masha Allah*."

"Yes Princess," added her dad, "hard to believe what an awful little kid you used to be."

Amirah sat up and smiled at her dad with raised eyebrows.

"Me! An awful kid?" declared Amirah, looking at him in surprise. "Why did you say that dad?"

"Ahh just remembering a few incidents," he said.

"Well Granny, I think I must be pretty special, you know why?" asked Amirah.

"Why dear?"

"Because I don't ever remember my dad getting angry with me and I'm fourteen years old," said Amirah smugly.

Granny laughed. "That's right love, but I remember one time when he nearly did."

"Which particular event are you referring to?" Adam smiled.

"The jacket and the haircut," said Granny matter-of-factly.

"What jacket and what haircut?" asked Amirah curiously.

Adam and Granny started to chuckle.

"Well, as I recall," started Granny, "you were about four years old."

"A really devoted daughter," smiled Adam.

"It was winter," said Granny, "and of course your dad always wore his sheep skin coat and when he came home…"

"He hung it on the coat stand in the hallway," put in Amirah.

"Right! Then one day when your dad had just come home, he went to have a nap and you were busy playing in your room."

"Mum, do you remember how she used to talk to herself?"

"I sure do. Cutest little thing you were, Amirah. You were busy playing 'schools' with your teddy bears. You had them all lined up like they were sitting in school, and you were teaching them how to read. Well anyway, I was cooking in the kitchen as I recall and like I say, your dad was resting, and you got your dad's coat and gave it a haircut. Now I don't know where you got the scissors from, but you snipped away at all the fur around the collar, right down to the second or third button."

"My poor coat," groaned Adam.

"After you finished your little job, you put the coat on the stand and went back to play. Then when your dad woke up. He got ready to go out and I heard him shout."

"Dad never shouts Granny."

"I know! I must say I nearly had a heart attack. I rushed into the hallway and there he was standing with the coat in his hand. He called you and you came rushing out. Before I could say anything, he asked you, 'What have you done to my coat?'" Granny imitated

Adam's gruff voice.

"What did I say Granny? I don't remember all these details."

"You smiled so sweetly and said, 'What a nice haircut! Now your nice coat is all pretty and tidy,'" said Granny in a squeaky little girly voice.

"Now, I could see the funny side of it, but I tried not to laugh. You were so innocent and sweet, and your dad was so funny holding that ragged thing in his hands. Then for some reason you got all pouty and said, 'Whatcha' shouting at me for daddy? I just gave your coat a haircut!' And then you turned around and went marching back into your room as dignified as could be."

"What did you do Dad?" asked Amirah, looking at him intently.

"Let your Granny tell the story Princess," said Adam reminiscing.

"Well, that just left me and your dad standing in the hallway and before I could say anything, he dropped the coat onto the floor and followed you into the room. He looked around quickly and found the scissors on the dressing table, grabbed your favorite teddy on his chair and started snipping away."

Amirah stared at Adam.

"Dad! How could you cut up my favorite teddy bear?" she laughed.

"Well, when your dad started snipping away at teddy, you ran over angrily and tried to grab him off your dad and he was pulling it and you were pulling at it, and I was standing in the doorway laughing. I thought, 'Any minute they're going to pull that old teddy apart.' You started screaming, 'That's my teddy Daddy!' and he's saying, 'I'm just giving him a haircut!' I think this went on for a few minutes until your dad loosened his hold and you and teddy went flying across the room. You jumped up and slipped teddy under your bed out of harm's way. Then your dad said, 'See! You don't like it when someone gives your teddy a haircut and I don't like it when you give my coat a haircut! Okay!' Then you shouted, 'Okay!' And your dad stomped out of the room, and you sat down on your bed with the biggest pout."

"I remember that Granny but I'm glad you reminded me of the details."

"Perfect kid hey Princess?" asked Adam cheekily.

"What happened after that," said Amirah, not wanting to comment.

"Well, you sat for a while, and I left you, but I watched from a distance. You went behind the chair in the living room and gathered up all the wool you'd cut from the coat and got a bottle of glue and you sat there, dear sweet little thing, and tried to glue all the wool back onto the coat."

"Yeah, Granny, I remember doing that."

"When your dad came out later, he was much calmer and by then you were asleep. He looked at his coat in the hallway and he picked it up. He was staring at it this way and that and then I heard him roar with laughter. I came through and I must say that coat looked a sight. I think we must have laughed a solid five minutes."

Amirah shook her head, "Well Dad, I did try to make up for it."

"Yes, you did."

"Whatever happened to that coat?" asked Amirah.

"Well, precious things like that can't be thrown away," said Adam. "Actually, I packed it, and it is in my blue suitcase."

"You mean you're bringing that tacky old coat to Egypt?" asked Granny.

"I couldn't leave it behind," said Adam with a smile.

"You know what Dad?"

"What Princess?"

"I brought my teddy too. You know, the one who had the haircut."

They all smiled and remembered together. Then without realizing it, the plane began its descent into Cairo airport.

CHAPTER 6

In Egypt

CAIRO

Amirah woke with a start. She looked around her and saw the unfamiliar room. Soft streaks of yellow from the streetlights below filtered through the closed green shutters. The walls were a pale yellow and the huge wardrobe, bed, and dressing table stood just as they had when generations before had woken and slept and lived their lives in the same place. The cotton quilt lay heavily on top of Amirah as she strained to see the room.

She could barely remember climbing the four flights of stairs, entering the flat and dropping into an exhausted heap on the bed.

Suddenly a loud and clear sound boomed out into the night. A husky male voice called *'Allahu Akbar'* and Amirah instantly knew it was time for *Fajr* Prayer. Just after one voice began calling the *'Adhan'*, another voice from another masjid started calling, then another and another. Before long, it sounded like a chorus, calling the people to wake up and pray.

Despite her tiredness she reached for her dressing down and went out to explore her new home. She had to wrestle a little with the door handle, but eventually she opened it and padded softly along the hallway to the living room. There she saw Adam putting on his sheepskin jacket and about to leave the flat.

"Just going down to the *masjid* to pray Princess. Won't be long."

Amirah nodded and went to find Granny, hugging herself to be warm. She knocked on Granny's door and it opened a little. Amirah knocked again and Granny came over and opened the door, wrapping Amirah in a bear hug.

"So, how's my girl today?"

"I'm Okay, *alhumdulillah*," answered Amirah.

"Are you ready to pray?"

"Yes, I've just prayed the *Sunnah*. What about you?" asked Granny.

"Give me a minute and I'll make *wudu*. Will you wait for me Granny?" asked Amirah.

"Of course. Hurry up then."

The bathroom was very simple. It had a wash basin and small square ceramic tiled bath. Everything was a faded white color and the tap on the wash basin continually dripped. Amirah tried to close the tap firmly, but it still leaked. She washed herself ready to pray and hurried back to Granny.

Granny's room was filled with bags and suitcases, but the room had the same kind of permanent look to it and made Amirah feel comfortable. Granny's room also had a balcony, and the glass doors and shutters were open. The branches of a Jasmine tree peaked over the cement wall of the balcony and its perfume filled the air.

"I like your room Granny."

"Me too, dear. Come on let's pray."

The growing morning light inched its way upward in the sky and flowed into the room casting little shadows on the walls and Granny and Amirah stood, knelt, and prostrated to the Lord thanking Him for all they had – and for each other.

CHAPTER 7

Memories

"What will we do today, Granny?" asked Amirah as she started shuffling around the bags and suitcases looking for things.

"Unpacking, I think. Aren't you tired dear?"

"I can't wait until we're settled, and we can get out and have a look around the place. When's Dad coming back?"

As soon as Amirah had finished her sentence the front door banged, and Adam came rushing inside in a whirl of energy.

"How was the *masjid* dear?" asked Granny, as she opened the bags, and started stacking clothes and books onto the bed ready to sort out.

"Fine *Alhumdulillah*. I got breakfast," he said eagerly with sheer happiness on his face.

"What did you buy at this time of day, Dad," asked Amirah, trying to peek into the bags.

"Bananas and apples!"

"I thought you said breakfast!" she cried. She stared at the fruit in disbelief.

"I think Amirah thought you meant *ful* beans, *falafel*, and nice fresh pita bread – things like that, dear," said Granny trying to soothe the situation.

"For breakfast?" exclaimed Adam. "The best thing in the morning is fruit. We've been eating fruit for breakfast since I can remember!"

"So, isn't it time for a change then?" asked Amirah, disappointed.

"But it's not healthy to eat heavy things like that in the morning," insisted Adam.

"And besides where will I get *ful* and what's-its-name from this time of day?"

"People buy it from stands in the street," said Granny. "I'm sure if you go to the corner of the main street you'll find it, *Insha Allah*," she added, winking at Amirah.

"And I'll eat an apple and a banana by the time you come back Dad! Promise!" said Amirah hopefully.

Adam mumbled something under his breath, grabbed three bananas and two apples, flung on his jacket, and opened the front door.

"Just so long as you appreciate me," said Adam, trying to appear stern. "But," he added, "I'm going for a run first and I'll get your *ful* and what's-its-name on the way back."

"Be careful dear," said Granny, feeling a bit worried, "you don't know the streets yet."

"Don't worry about me, Mum! What is there to know?"

With that, Adam closed the door and the sound of his footsteps bounding down the stairs echoed through the building.

"Allah protect him," said Granny quietly.

She and Amirah started unpacking.

"Granny."

"Yes dear."

"We have a lot of memories, don't we."

"Oh yes, we certainly do," said Granny, as she stacked piles of neatly folded clothes in the cupboard and drawers.

"I'm scared."

"Of what dear?" Granny stopped what she was doing and looked at Amirah.

"Of forgetting."

"You mean forgetting your memories?" Amirah nodded her head and sat down on the giant solid bed. It creaked. Granny put down the pile of clothes in her hands and sat beside her. Her soft gentle hands brushed the hair away from Amirah's face and she cradled her chin in her hand.

"Memories live inside us dear. We might forget them for a time but they're there and when we see or hear something that reminds us of them, they come back to our mind, and we enjoy them all over again."

"But what will I do if I get so full up that the memories get pushed way to the back of my mind?"

"Our minds are much, much bigger than you could ever imagine! Why, we don't even use a tiny percentage of the mind's capabilities! Don't you worry about that. The funny thing about the mind and memories is that the more you try to grasp hold of them, the more they seem to slip away. If we just let them go, they come back when we need them."

"Really Granny?"

"Really."

Amirah smiled and Granny gave her a long hug.

"Just let your thoughts wander around and take you wherever they want to go, dear. All your life is in here and here."

Granny pointed to Amirah's head and heart.

"And there's plenty more space for new memories."

"Yeah Granny. I think we're going to have lots of new memories here. I can't wait to see Egypt. I want my life to start."

"It's already started! You're making memories all the time. I have an idea. Why don't you keep a diary and write down all the special things that happen. That way you can look back and recall your memories much more easily. What do you think?"

"I think that's a great idea."

Amirah rummaged around in one of the suitcases until she found teddy with the haircut, a photo of The Retreat, and a notebook.

"This will do Granny." Amirah smiled.

"That is perfect dear! Come on, we have chores to do. Let's get on with it."

CHAPTER 8

A New Memory

"Granny! This floor is driving me mad!"

"What's the matter?" asked Granny, as she rushed from the kitchen into the bathroom.

One of Amirah's chores was to clean the bathroom and wash the floor.

"I've never had to mop a floor like this!"

Amirah was wearing her plastic apron and rubber gloves and chasing the water on the bathroom floor around with a rubber mop.

"Isn't the water supposed to just automatically go down the drain Granny?" Amirah was quite exasperated.

"No need to get so upset about mopping a floor dear," said Granny, leaning on the door frame watching Amirah scoop water toward the drain only to see it flowing away back toward her.

"But aren't the floors supposed to be designed that the water goes down the drain!" Amirah almost shouted these words.

"Well, yes, theoretically they're supposed to, I guess," said Granny smiling.

She could usually see the funny side of things.

They were interrupted by the doorbell ringing frantically! Granny and Amirah stared at each other and ran to the door.

Ding! Dong! Dong! Dong! Dong! Granny opened the door.

"Mum!" panted Adam.

He stumbled into the room and collapsed onto a chair. He didn't even take off his comfy trainers. His pants were torn, and his hands were grazed. He mopped at them with some tissues.

"Dad! Are you Okay?" asked Amirah concerned.

Adam closed his eyes, trying to control himself yet hiding a small smile.

"What on earth happened?" demanded Granny, getting some water and a cloth. She saw that smile.

Adam sat up and opened his eyes halfway. His blonde hair was tousled, and he was sweating profusely.

"I nearly got killed!" he said, still trying to catch his breath.

Amirah's eyes widened. "Not death again!" she thought. "Do you want a glass of water Dad?"

"Yes, please Princess. Oh, what a day and it's still only morning."

"Adam dear. What are you doing running around this time of day?" asked Granny, giving him a sideways glance while wiping his face.

"Like I said before I left, I went for a jog. All in the way of getting little red nose over here some *ful* and what's-its-name! It's such a beautiful morning I had to go for a run."

Granny started to smile. "And where, my dear son, did you run to in the middle of this gigantic city? And you don't even know your way around yet!"

"All around the buildings here. I wanted to check

out the area. I went down this great avenue with trees on either side and the air was so cool and fresh. Well, I just kept running."

"Dad, hurry up and tell us what happened," said Amirah, getting impatient.

She was still wearing her plastic apron and rubber gloves.

"I'm hungry. Can't talk," said Adam with a twinkle in his eye.

"Nothing's changed," grumbled Amirah, getting up to find some fruit for him.

"Dad," said Amirah from the kitchen, "there's only about a kilo of bananas here on the bench. You didn't get breakfast!"

"That'll do," Adam called out.

Granny chuckled.

Adam laughed, "You should be glad your hardworking son is still here to tell the story," said Adam, peeling and swallowing bananas.

"I wish you'd get on and tell it then," said Amirah. "Okay Dad, you've eaten. Now come on and tell us what happened!"

"Well Princess, I found myself on the other side

of this road. I remember crossing it when the traffic was light but when I came to cross it again the traffic was surging. I kept waiting for the lights to change and they did, but the cars kept on coming. 'This is ridiculous,' I thought. 'I'll be here all day.' There were about four or five lanes of traffic, and I kept jogging on the spot to keep my blood moving. Then I saw some young fellows approaching the road. Of course, they were going to cross over, and I thought I'd cross with them but before I could get myself in gear they were dancing between the cars and all I could do was stare in wonder. I knew I could never do that, and I had this awful feeling that I'd be here for the rest of my life!"

"You're telling us Dad that you couldn't even cross the road?" pointed out Amirah cheekily.

"Just you wait. Your turn will come," said Adam with a tone in his voice. "I'd like to see you skip between these cars."

"They'd stop for me," said Amirah smartly.

"What makes you think that?" inquired Adam.

"Because I'm a girl and chivalry is still alive and well over here. Granny told me that herself, didn't you Granny?"

"Yes dear, I did."

Granny and Amirah started staring at Adam to get him to complete the story. Amirah rolled her eyes.

"Well," said Adam, sitting up straighter. "Do you know how long I stood at the curb? Do you have any idea how long I stood jogging on the spot, staring at streams of traffic wondering how I was going to get home?"

"You must have been quite a spectacle dear," commented Granny. "People over here don't jog, at least not on a main street."

"Oh well, learning all the time," said Adam. "Any way after about half an hour I'd had enough."

"Half an hour!" said Amirah, laughing out loud. "Poor Dad, you must have worn the foot path out jogging on it all that time."

"Now dear," said Granny, "you must sympathize with your dad, he's had a trying morning." She grinned.

"I'm so glad I wasn't there," remarked Amirah, laughing till she almost cried. "I would have died from embarrassment."

"Settle down, don't you want to hear how your dear old dad was nearly killed today?"

"Yes, yes, go on," said Amirah, drying her tears.

"After all that time, things started to get blurry and the buses, cars and taxis and donkey carts too, all became a fuzz and I so desperately wanted to get home that I thought I'd just take my chances. So, I jogged up and down the street a few times and thought I'd approach it fresh. I went and bought myself a juice and then I got the idea to take some side streets and come the back way. So, I jogged up the road and into a smaller street. Anyway, when I approached that street, I felt more confident. At last, I could see some of the road and I stepped out onto it and then there was a screech of tires and shouts from all around and I felt myself flying into the air and suddenly surrounded by people."

"Oh Dad! You got hit?"

"Just a bit, but it's okay."

"How come you didn't see the car coming Adam?" asked Granny disbelievingly.

"Car? It was a small truck! Well, I just, well, you know.."

"Come on Dad."

"For a second, I forgot I'm in Egypt and I looked the wrong way to check if any cars were coming and I couldn't see any because they were all coming the other way."

Adam put his head down feeling a bit ashamed of having been so foolish. Granny and Amirah felt his embarrassment but still laughed out loud.

"Hey Granny, aren't *mahrams* supposed to help you cross the road? I'll think I'll pass on that service!"

"Me too," joined in Granny. "By the way dear, where did the car, I mean the truck, hit you?"

"Well, you know, it was kind of, ummm … from behind."

"That's good. You'll be right then."

Granny gave him a playful slap on the leg and laughed all the way to the kitchen.

"I'm so sorry you got hurt Dad," said Amirah more seriously. "Are you really all right?"

Adam paused.

"I can see the funny side of it," said Adam, but I tell you the worst thing was not knowing how to cross the road. It seems there is an art to it, an art I'll have to learn. I never thought I'd be afraid to cross a road."

He shook his head disbelievingly.

Adam reached over and hugged Amirah. "I wish

you'd been there with me today," he said smiling.

"I'm glad I wasn't!"

"You're just kidding, aren't you?"

"Yeah, Dad. I would have helped you cross the road."

Adam tossed a cushion at her and then asked her, "Hey Princess."

"Yeah Dad."

"Are you ever going to change?"

"Nope, never."

Adam looked at Amirah and felt frightened deep inside. She was growing up. He wanted to cling to her childishness; her innocence, for as long as he could.

"Say *Insha Allah*," he said with a gentle smile.

"*Insha Allah*," Amirah beamed.

Adam pulled himself off the chair, and winced a little when he stood up straight. Still dabbing at his grazed face, he went to the bathroom to take a shower.

"Oh, by the way Dad."

"Yeah what?" asked Adam grimacing.

"Thanks for the new memory! It's a beauty." She smiled and took her notebook and wrote 'Diary' on the front cover.

CHAPTER 9

Out on the Town

"Adam dear," said Granny. "Amirah and I are going out to do some shopping.

Granny leaned over and opened the living-room window to let in the sunlight. A few birds on a nearby tree flew off at the sound of the scraping wood as Granny stretched open the green shutters.

"The sky is a bit grey," said Adam peering out the window. "Will you be able to manage without me?"

"Don't worry, we won't be long," reassured Granny.

She and Amirah were standing ready to go out. Amirah had been nagging her for some time that they needed this and that for the house and so Granny eventually agreed they should go shopping.

"You sure you won't get lost?" asked Adam through sleepy eyes.

"Remember, I know my way around," said Granny who had visited Egypt a few times throughout the years. "We're off to Roxy."

"I've heard of that area. It's not far from here," noted Adam.

"I believe so," said Granny, picking up her bag and putting on her shoes. "Many of the buildings were built some years ago and have lovely designs and architecture. Not like the rectangular boxes they build now."

"Oh! I can't wait!" said Amirah, who had been waiting for some time. "We're going to have a day on the town!"

In her excitement she didn't notice the yellowish haze falling over the already grey sky.

"Just be careful," warned Adam. He yawned.

"Don't worry," they both said in unison.

Amirah rolled her eyes. "We know how to cross the road, Dad!"

Adam chuckled quietly, and stifling another yawn, chose to ignore that statement. He went quietly through to his room.

"We'll see," he said, half to himself.

He was soon sound asleep and didn't hear their giggles and laughter as the door shut behind them.

※

Standing on the side of the road, Amirah looked in wonder at the number of BMWs, Mercedes, and all kinds of fancy cars cruising along.

"Why do we have to catch a bus?" asked Amirah, feeling embarrassed as one after another beaten-up buses passed them by, ignoring their waves to stop.

"At least we could ride in a taxi," she suggested, half begging.

There were so many people and so much commotion that Amirah felt a bit lost. The buses didn't stop for them. It was almost as if they didn't exist – they were being ignored.

"They're not very friendly Granny."

"Who dear?" asked Granny, trying to wave down another bus.

"The people," said Amirah.

"Which people do you mean?"

"Oh, just – everyone. They don't smile or anything."

"Amirah, you're looking at the wrong people. Egyptian people are very friendly. If there are a few who are not, it doesn't mean they all are."

A strong gust of wind nearly knocked Amirah into Granny.

"The wind is getting quite strong Granny."

Amirah turned her face toward the sky. It was a brownish, yellowish, grayish color.

Granny stood strong and straight on the roadside, patiently flagging down buses as her long jilbab and scarf fluttered around in the rising wind.

"Why don't they stop?" asked Amirah, starting to feel annoyed.

She had to quickly step out of the way as a Mercedes was backing out of its parking place. It didn't even beep or anything, it just kept coming and Amirah had to jump. She stood closer to Granny, wishing they were on their way.

"One will," said Granny, "eventually...If the bus is full, it won't stop. Simple."

Holding onto Granny's arm, Amirah stared at the whirling traffic and imagined how her dad must have felt trying to cross the road. Looking at the road then at big red buses, green buses, coaches, minibuses, cars, taxis, motorbikes, donkey carts, bicycles, police cars and lorries – she felt dizzy. And it wasn't just the traffic, it was the way they pushed and shoved; it was like there were no road laws. Nevertheless, she never saw any cars collide.

Just a little up from where they were an old woman was trying to venture out into the traffic. She wanted to cross the road. She must have been very old. The cars whizzed by. There was no way she could safely cross the road. Amirah felt like they should do something. Then a police officer came out of nowhere. He spoke to the old woman then walked into the traffic. He held up his hand and brought the traffic to a dramatic halt. While holding the cars and trucks and taxis at bay with one hand, he gestured to the old woman to cross the road. She tottered out and crossed safely. Her old legs moved slowly, but nobody said anything, nobody beeped their horn. When she was safely across the road, the police officer waved the cars on, and everything returned to normal.

They were standing on the side of a large road. There were four lanes of traffic on one side and four lanes on the other. The lanes were separated by a beautiful garden of grass, palm trees, and an assortment of flowers and bushes in the middle. Men with worn-out tired faces stood dangerously close to the traffic on the outside of the traffic island, sweeping the sides of the road with ancient brooms, and using pieces of cardboard to scoop up the dirt into rubber buckets. The sky was a pasty grey color and Amirah wondered if she'd ever see the blue sky again. The exhaust fumes nearly choked her, and she covered her mouth and nose with her sleeve to keep out the noxious smoke.

Despite the smoky surrounds, the garden was pretty. Amidst the rushing traffic she saw one expensive car slow down next to an old man who was cleaning the street and the driver gave him some money in his hand, then sped off again among the whirring body of traffic.

The poor man's face shone with happiness and his comrades glared at the car that had chosen not to give to them.

"Did you see that dear?" commented Granny, pointing to the poor man holding the money in his hand. "There are always good people," said Granny.

"I guess."

Amirah was wondering why the man in the car hadn't given some money to all the men. Perhaps it would cause a fight.

Amirah turned to the buses again, hoping one would stop for them. She stared in amazement as men ran and chased the buses down the road. There were businessmen with suits and ties holding briefcases and looking important. Then there were workers wearing *jalabeyas*, with *ship-ship* on their calloused feet. But they all had one thing in common, the buses never stopped for any of them. Whenever a man wanted to get onto a bus, it never came to a complete halt, but merely slowed down to allow the panting passenger to 'jump' on board.

"Will they stop for us?" asked Amirah, wondering if she would have to run and jump on the bus like the men were doing.

"Don't be such a worrier," smiled Granny.

Another bus whirled past, puffing out acrid black smoke.

"That's disgusting!" said Amirah, holding her nose again and drawing her bag tightly to her. The noise of the traffic, the continual exhaust fumes being flung in her face, the strong gusts of dusty wind, and the crowded streets all made her feel a bit dizzy. Her feeling of excitement had vanished. She wanted to go home. She was just about to open her mouth and insist when Granny said, "Here we are!"

At last, a bus stopped. Amirah found herself half dragged, half pushed onto the overcrowded little bus.

"Hold on here," said Granny, pointing to a pole in front of the seats. Amirah was sullen but she obeyed. She leaned close to Granny and asked, "Why did the bus stop for us?"

"Because we're ladies," said Granny.

Amirah nodded and muttered something to herself then gazed silently at the assortment of people before her. She still thought they should have taken a taxi. A young man jumped up and gave his seat to Granny who nodded her head in thanks, smiled, and sat down. Amirah found herself standing next to two women. One was tall and well-built with a tight-fitting skirt and jacket. She wore her hijab pinned close to her head and her hands were filled with gold rings and bracelets. Amirah tried not to stare but the woman moved her hands a lot as she spoke. Amirah couldn't understand what was being said. She felt foolish to have been learning Arabic for so long, and yet she was still hardly able to understand a thing the woman was saying. The woman's large strong hands punctuated her sentences and the flash of gold, the lilt in her voice, and her demeanor made her look like a lady of strength. "Ladies must be tough to ride buses," thought Amirah with a sigh.

It wasn't long before Granny stood up, grabbed Amirah's arm, and hoisted her down the three steps onto the safety of the pavement. The bus rattled off; black smoke filling the air. Staring after it, Amirah wondered how they ever allowed themselves to get onto such an unsafe vehicle in the first place.

"Come on," said Granny enthusiastically, "follow me!" Filled with excitement, Granny headed off into the crowds of people. Amirah followed behind still feeling moody and wishing that Granny would slow down. The wind pushed Amirah along. She struggled to keep her balance as she was pushed by passersby. Worse, she had to dodge rocks on the pavement, climbing up and down steps connecting the pavement to driveways. All the time Amirah had to be close to Granny who seemed to be racing down the street.

Everywhere Amirah looked, there were crowds of people. It was difficult to navigate her way down the pavement because it wasn't level and the path in front of nearly every building seemed to have its own design. So sometimes she had to step onto the road to get around a parked car or a large dip going down beside a garage opening. She also had to avoid the litter and dirt. It became harder and harder for Amirah to concentrate on where Granny was, let alone trying to see in the shop windows.

CHAPTER 10

Taxi!

Granny was standing in the entrance of yet another shop. She turned around and said, "Come on slowcoach!" in a loud voice.

Amirah imagined a dozen people turning to stare at her. Granny was smiling as Amirah made her way up to her.

"Why are people staring at me all the time?" whispered Amirah. She was getting fed up.

"You look like a foreigner dear. Don't worry. Just keep going on your way. People are curious, that's all."

Granny walked into the shop and started examining dishes, plates, and trays, but Amirah refused to go inside and insisted on waiting at the doorway.

"Now come on Amirah! I don't want you to get lost," said Granny, poking her head around the corner of the doorway. "Stay within my sight."

Granny was worried. Amirah didn't budge.

The busy noisy traffic, the crowded pavement with people pushing and charging in front of her, the uneven ground, and the looks and whispers she saw and heard as people stumbled past her had all made Amirah feel more and more awkward and uncomfortable. She really wanted to be at home. No matter how hard Amirah tried, she had this growing feeling of self-consciousness and she wished there was a big hole somewhere where she could just jump in and hide from everything.

Amirah stubbornly remained outside the shop while Granny, beginning to feel vexed, kept searching for the dishes she wanted.

Just when Amirah was about to confront Granny and demand they go home, an extra strong gust of wind blew her *hijab* up over her face and she spent a few minutes trying to untangle herself. She had never felt so stupid and embarrassed in all her life.

Granny rushed out of the shop.

"Hold on dear," said Granny, putting her shopping bags down and trying to help Amirah.

"I can manage," she snapped.

When she finally arranged her *hijab,* her face was bright red, and she was pushing back tears. People were staring at her and smiling. She did look rather funny, but it wasn't the time to laugh.

"I still have a few more shops to go to, dear. Then we can stop for a sandwich.

That was it. Amirah couldn't take it anymore.

"I don't want a sandwich Granny! I just want to go home!"

"But Amirah, you're the one who wanted to go shopping in the first place."

Amirah knew that was true but there was no way she would admit it now.

"Yeah maybe, but now I want to go home."

"That's no way to talk young lady," said Granny, getting red in the face.

"And," added Amirah, "I don't want to go home on one of those broken-down buses! I've had enough of buses. I want to go home in a taxi!"

"Indeed!" said Granny, who stormed off down the street mumbling something under her breath about 'taxis……snobbish attitude…..buses are good enough for me……'

Amirah watched Granny on the side of the road trying to flag down a taxi. She was carrying a load of shopping bags and her clothes were flying around. She had to catch the end of her *hijab* to stop it flying up over her face. Amirah started to feel a bit sorry she'd been so rude, but she didn't know what to do. Granny's face, that was usually so friendly, was set in a stern expression. It wasn't the time to say anything now. What a terrible day! She wished her dad was there.

The sky turned dark, and the wind began to pick up again. Plastic bags were flying down the street like so many balloons let go at once. They would have looked pretty if they weren't surrounded by dust and smoke. Amirah was scanning the road looking for a taxi. Her eyes were half shut to keep the sand out and she strained to see a black and white car parked on the side of the street with the rear door open. She started to run and caught Granny by the arm.

"Come on Granny! I've found us a taxi!"

Granny didn't need any more convincing. She followed Amirah and they both collapsed into the back seat of the car.

The driver was sitting calmly eating a sandwich. Determined to be good and show Granny she was sorry, Amirah took the initiative and leaned forward and said in her best Arabic, "*Emirate al Oboor, min fadlak.*"

Then with a satisfied look on her face she sat back and waited for the taxi to set off. Granny was busy arranging her bags and had settled in the back seat next to the window. The driver didn't move.

"Maybe he didn't understand me," thought Amirah to herself.

"*Emirate al Oboor, min fadlak,*" she repeated, saying each word loudly and clearly.

Once again, she settled back in the seat and tried to relax after the tiresome day. Again, the driver didn't move or show any signs of starting the car.

He stared at them through the rear-view mirror with a puzzled expression. Granny looked at the man in the mirror, then looked at Amirah. She put her hand to her face and covered her mouth. Try as she might, she couldn't stop the burst of laughter from coming. Amirah looked at the man, opened her mouth to repeat her request then started to feel uneasy. With a sick feeling in her stomach she turned to Granny, and said, "Oh Granny! I don't think this is a taxi!"

"Neither do I, dear!" whispered Granny, trying to stifle a fit of the giggles.

"What should we do now?" asked Amirah in horror and mortification as a woman emerged from a nearby shop and climbed into the front seat. She glanced behind at Granny and Amirah and said something to the driver. Then both stared straight ahead, neither saying a word.

"I'm out of here," said Granny.

She was beginning to push Amirah out of the back seat, when a young man began climbing into the back of the car. He got out to let them out and stood there scratching his head. Granny and Amirah scrambled out of the car and started to walk quickly up the street. Amirah felt like she would die of embarrassment. This couldn't possibly be happening to her! After some way, Granny stopped and turned around to look at the car and the people in it. They were sitting in the car in fits of laughter and there were people around them in the street pointing and laughing.

It was then that Granny started to laugh. She couldn't help it.

Scowling and determined not to see the funny side of anything, Amirah followed Granny who promptly flagged down a taxi. A real one this time!

Just when they were getting into the taxi, the sky turned black, and the wind blew so strongly that the taxi driver had to hold his foot on the brake and put on the hand brake to stop the car from being blown off the road.

"If I didn't know better," said Granny, "I'd say this is a hurricane!"

"The perfect end to a perfect day," said Amirah drearily.

She sank down into the back seat and closed her eyes.

CHAPTER 11
Windstorm! What Next?

The two unhappy shoppers climbed the stairs to the flat. What should have taken ten minutes by car to get home, had taken hours. The traffic had come to a standstill, and they needed to wait for the wind to die down. Now weary, miserable, and with Amirah determined to stonewall, they entered the flat. Nothing could have prepared them for what they saw.

The wind was still blowing strongly outside but not as bad as before. It had done its work though and the flat was covered in a thick layer of fine dust. Granny stared at the floor in dismay and saw their footprints as clearly as if they were walking on the beach. She rushed over and closed the window and the shutter that had let in all the dust.

"Oh my! Oh my! *Alhumdulilah* for everything," she said quietly.

Amirah just stood there, her eyes scanning the flat. Everything, absolutely everything was covered in dust and the air was thick. She felt like she was choking.

Granny wandered through the flat not knowing what to say or even to think. She went into Adam's room. There he lay flat on his back, with his head tilted back, snoring loudly. He was sound asleep. He was also covered by a layer of fine dust.

"My goodness, that man could sleep through anything," she said. She reached down and shook him hard.

"Adam! Adam! Wake up!"

"What? Yeah Mum. You're home now?"

"Didn't you hear the windstorm?"

"What windstorm?" he asked, confused.

Then he started coughing and spluttering and Granny hurried to the kitchen to get him some water. He got up and walked into the living room. He opened and closed his eyes a few times and looked at Amirah sitting on the chair – her face blank.

"What on earth?" he said.

Adam stood scratching his head trying to decide if this was just a bad dream. His hair and beard were covered in dust and even the tip of his nose. The dust had settled on him when he was asleep, making him look like some kind of statue. If he had shaken his clothes, dust would have gone flying everywhere.

Amirah stared at him. The humiliation and ordeal of the day seemed to fade away and all she could see was her dad looking the funniest she had ever seen him, but she still found it hard to laugh.

"I think you'd better look in the mirror," suggested Amirah.

"You're joking," said Adam, running his finger over the glass drawing a picture of Amirah with a miserable face.

"That mirror is really dirty," said Adam, rubbing away at it now.

For as hard as he rubbed, he still got a strange reflection back of himself.

"That's not the mirror dear. It's you!" said Granny. "You're a sorry sight. You're absolutely covered in dust."

Adam strained his eyes into the mirror and began brushing dust off his eyebrows and beard. Amirah started to smile despite herself.

"Well, there's no use dusting and cleaning now. It's better to let the dust settle and we'll clean everything tomorrow. Let's just clean up the beds and the table and what we really need today," stated Granny.

"Who's going to clean everything tomorrow?" asked Amirah, feeling quite overwhelmed. She couldn't imagine herself cleaning the flat after this had happened.

"All of us!" said Adam and Granny together.

"But can't we get one of those ladies who come to clean?"

Amirah stared at her hands and remembered the rubber mop in the bathroom.

"We're perfectly capable of cleaning our own home, dear," said Granny, who was still a bit stern with Amirah after today's episode.

"Well, I'm going to bed," announced Amirah. Without another word she got up and left the room.
The wind had died down.

"Your dad and I are going down to the shops. We'll be back soon," Granny called out.

Amirah didn't answer. She wasn't afraid in the slightest bit to be alone in the house. It would be nice to have some time on her own for a change.

CHAPTER 12

Just a Bathroom Drain

The front door closed quietly, and Amirah nestled into her bed with a book. She ignored her dusty surroundings and tried to forget the events of the day. It wasn't too long before she fell into a deep, but troubled sleep.

Thoughts of whirring traffic, smoke, laughs and sniggers, Granny's stern face, and a roaring wind made her toss and turn. She woke up with a start, trying to figure out where she was. She rubbed her eyes and breathed in more dust, all the while straining her eyes to see out of the dusty window. The sun was almost set, and she couldn't hear any noise in the flat.

"Dad and Granny must still be at the shops," she thought.

Amirah reached over to turn on her bedside lamp, but the bulb had blown and there was no light. She tiptoed over the carpet to turn on the main light and midway across the room she stopped still. The whole room started to shake. At first, she thought that, having just woken up, she was merely feeling dizzy. But then she noticed the picture on the wall jiggling around. The light hanging down from the center of the ceiling started to sway from side to side.

This was an earthquake! A thousand thoughts rushed through her mind. The building had 24 floors and they were on the third. Their building was surrounded by other buildings just as tall. Should she run out of the flat, and if so, should she run up to the top of the building or down to the street? Would the building collapse? Why didn't Granny and Dad come back? Amirah wanted to run in every direction, but she couldn't move from her place. She was stuck there as if her feet were sealed with cement. She stood silently in wide-eyed terror as the whole building continued to tremble.

"Oh Allah! Don't leave me even for a second."
The words rose from the depths of her soul.

There was a loud crash, a bang, and stomping footsteps. Someone screamed! Amirah stood frozen in her place.

"How can I save myself if I can't even move," she thought in desperation.

The ceiling light continued to swing frantically above her head. A vase fell off the desk and crashed into a thousand pieces on the floor. After what seemed like ages, the earthquake hushed. The horrible roaring noise stopped, and the building no longer moved, but the ceiling light continued to sway for a while. Amirah was still locked in her spot on the carpet, her eyes wide with fear.

Then the door flung open, and Adam ran into the room. He scooped her up in his arms and carried her through to the living room as if she were a little child again.

"Are you all right Princess?" He was panting. He never panted.

"I don't know," was all Amirah could say.

Adam sat down on the couch and held her close and rocked her until she stopped shaking. His hands were shaking as he stroked her head.

"Where's Granny?" asked Amirah once she had settled down.

"Oh well, she is, well, still downstairs. There is an ambulance coming."

"What?" Amirah sat up straight with wide eyes.

"Why does Granny need an ambulance?"

"She fell over when the earthquake struck. She got a shock and tripped over some stairs. She has hurt her leg. The ambulance is for someone else, not Granny. There are people with her downstairs. One of them is a doctor. *Masha Allah* the Egyptians are very kind."

Amirah jumped up. "I'm okay Dad. We must go down and help Granny!"

"If you're okay, we can go. I'm so sorry I left you alone," said Adam.

"It's okay Dad. I'm big now." She didn't feel big. She wanted to sound brave. She was still shaking inside.

"Dad will there be another earthquake?" asked Amirah quietly.

"I don't know, Princess," said Adam, looking lost. "I don't know but maybe there will be. It's not uncommon to have more tremors. Come on then, let's go."

When they got downstairs, Granny was sitting in a chair surrounded by women who were talking to her, comforting her, and giving her drinks. Amirah rushed over and gave her a big hug.

With tears in her eyes, she said, "Are you okay Granny? I'm sorry. I'm really sorry."

Granny nodded and smiled and patted Amirah's back and hugged her too.

"It's all right dear. It's been a difficult day, hasn't it?"

"What happened?" asked Amirah.

There were people everywhere she looked. A satellite dish had fallen to the ground, and everything appeared to be out of place.

Everything was in a whirl. She felt dizzy like she might faint. Some people looked scared, some looked angry, some looked calm.

Amirah put her head down. The doctor in the crowd had already checked Granny.

"Your leg is not broken," he said in perfect English. "Don't worry Madam. This tight bandage will be enough."

Granny nodded and smiled, and Adam and the doctor helped Granny upstairs.

※

Bright and early the following morning, Amirah woke to the sound of banging and scraping. She got up and walked through the settled dust and went to the living-room where she saw Adam with all the windows open and even the balcony doors and shutters, and he was pounding furniture, fluffing up cushions, sweeping, dusting, and mopping.

"How's things today, Princess?"

"Not too bad."

"Well, come on, dig in and start to help. Granny is resting in bed, and I told her that you and I will do all the cleaning. Isn't that right?"

Amirah nodded but still stood there.

"You're in charge of the kitchen and the bathroom," he announced matter-of-factly.

Amirah's heart sank. She just wished all this would go away. The dust, the accident, the embarrassment, the earthquake. Just go away.

"Make it snappy," said Adam. "And put a smile on your face while you're at it! Be grateful you're alive and have a place to live in."

Amirah didn't answer. She got changed into working clothes, put on her plastic apron and rubber gloves, and headed for the bathroom.

She looked at the dust. It was ingrained in every nook and cranny. This would take her ages. She sighed. Then Adam started to sing. For some reason he was in a good mood and his voice was loud and clear and spread warmth through the whole house. The banging, pounding, and splashing in the living-room continued.

"I bet the neighbors can hear," thought Amirah, feeling embarrassed again.

She wiped and scrubbed and arranged everything in the bathroom till it shone. Last was the floor. Amirah filled a bucket with hot soapy water and poured in a few drops of disinfectant and then splashed it over the floor.

Then she started pushing the water toward the drain as she had the other day. To her amazement the water flowed quickly and easily straight down the drain and disappeared.

"What on earth?" she said out loud.

"What's up Princess?" asked Adam as he stood in the doorway.

Amirah looked amazed as the water ran down the drain.

"Dad, you don't understand," she said in earnest. "The other day when I was cleaning, I had to push the water uphill to get it to go down the drain and then today it just flows down. It's almost like, well, that the floor is turned in the other direction."

She said these last words slowly with a dawning realization of what had happened.

"That is amazing," said Adam. He, too, stood and watched the water flow easily down the drain.

"It must have been the earthquake!" he commented.

"The building really did move," said Amirah with wide eyes. "The building must be in a different position than it was yesterday before the earthquake. Dad!"

She put her hands up to show the angle of the building standing in one position and then tilted them slightly to the right to indicate how it had changed its position.

"Granny! Do you know what happened? The building isn't straight anymore!" called out Amirah as she ran out the bathroom door.

CHAPTER 13
Battle of the Wills

Amirah sat with her chin on her books staring out the window. Flecks of dust danced in the light that cast a glow across the room. Granny was busy dusting the furniture and arranging things. She was always engrossed in whatever she did. Watching her made Amirah feel more tired.

"Have you finished that essay yet?" asked Granny, casting a sideways glance at her.

"Nearly."

"I think we have to email your work back to your teacher by tomorrow, isn't that right, dear?"

"Something like that."

Granny looked at Amirah.

"What's wrong Princess?"

"I'm tired of staying home. All I do is study, do housework, play netball at the club, and watch TV. My life is boring."

"You'll start school in September, *insha Allah*, but there's no need to just sit around doing nothing until then," said Granny.

Granny was standing beside the window with her head a little inclined to the right. She was thinking how pretty Amirah looked and how grown up she had become.

"Aunty Shadiya is coming around tomorrow," Granny reminded Amirah. "And she and her daughter are going to take you out. So, cheer up."

Granny looked hopeful. Amirah sighed and started chewing on her pen.

"Her daughter is a few years older than me and thinks I'm just a kid."

"You'll make more friends, dear. It takes time. Have you emailed your friends in Australia?"

"Yeah."

"Just keep yourself busy until school starts and then you'll see things will be different. It's never easy settling into a new country. Everything takes time."

Granny moved toward the window and looked out over the horizon. All she could see was buildings; rectangular, brownish-colored buildings.

"Granny."

"Yes, dear."

"Why doesn't Dad let me go downstairs by myself? He thinks I'm still a baby."

"Your dad is just worried about you. It's normal that fathers want to protect their kids."

Granny came to sit on the armchair next to the desk where Amirah was sitting.

"But downstairs there are a lot of shops and nice gardens to walk around. Really Granny I think it's a bit silly that I'm fourteen and still can't go down by myself."

"Look dear," said Granny, giving Amirah a hug. "Your dad is adjusting too and he's afraid for you. We're new here and we don't know how things work – I mean, who good people are and who's not to be trusted. Maybe you're a bit too trusting," suggested Granny.

"I don't trust anyone!" exclaimed Amirah, sitting up. "Is that all? Is it just because you both think I'm too trusting?"

Amirah couldn't believe her ears. They really did think she was still a kid! This was getting ridiculous.

"Really Granny. Can't you both give me credit for having more maturity than that?"

Granny watched Amirah as she jumped off the chair and started stomping around the room, protesting how mature she really was, while mumbling heatedly under her breath. When Amirah had finished stomping, she came to rest all red in the face.

"Do you honestly believe that makes me think you're mature, dear?" asked Granny, looking at her over the top of her spectacles.

Amirah didn't know what to say so she went back to her desk.

"I've got some work to do, Granny. I'll talk to you later."

She went through to her room.

※

Amirah sat quietly on her bed and stared out the window. The tree outside was growing beautiful red flowers and the fine leaves danced gently in the breeze.

"How different life is over here," she thought. "How different I am."

Her mind went back to their arrival in Cairo and how excited she'd been. She'd been to visit a few places but the trip to Roxy and the taxi and the windstorm now sent a shudder down her spine whenever she thought about it.

She'd been struggling to get some freedom. She wasn't really sure what she wanted to do. She just knew she didn't feel happy. Perhaps if she went out more, had more friends, perhaps then she'd feel happier. She felt alone. She felt scared. She felt she was losing herself; that she was changing and that she couldn't keep up with the changes. She also felt for the first time that Granny and her dad seemed so far away from her. She wanted to rush through to them and hug them both and be their 'Princess' again but she couldn't; she didn't know how to. She wished her mum was there.

Tears filled her eyes, spilling over and leaving two rivulets as they trickled down her cheeks. "Mum," she said quietly to herself. How nice it would be to have her there; to have a mum that she could talk to; someone who would understand. She put her head down and scribbled with a pen on some paper.

"*Alhumdulillah* for everything," she said softly to herself.

Then she remembered the box of knick-knacks her dad had given her when they arrived in Egypt.

"This is some stuff that belonged to your mum, and I think it might be useful for you now," he'd said. She rummaged through her wardrobe and found it under the box of schoolbooks. She had been waiting to look through it. She wasn't quite sure why she was waiting. It was a large square cardboard box that had been decorated with different kinds of material until it looked like a patchwork box instead of a patchwork quilt. There were notebooks and little books with hard covers and each one was decorated in a unique way with colored fabric, bits of paper and shiny material. The handwriting was a bit like her own. When she looked closer, she found the notebooks were mostly made from re-cycled paper.

"That's my mum, the environmentalist!" smiled Amirah.

She picked up one of the hard-covered notebooks and opened it at random. She was eager to read all the quotes and notes her mother had written. As she read, she began to see life through her mother's eyes. The beautiful meaning of the words struck Amirah and a feeling of something greater than happiness rose in her heart. Her mum had written those words! They were important to her. After a while, her heart felt much more at peace, and she put the notebooks gently back in the patchwork box.

"Mum needed to be inspired sometimes, just like me," thought Amirah.

She was determined to write down her own memories and thoughts and keep them alongside her mother's.

※

"I'm home!" called out Adam.

He bounded into the living room with a beaming face and held out a plastic bag to Granny.

"I've got some *ful* and what's-its-name," he said happily.

"Thanks son," said Granny quietly.

"Well, you know what happened last time I tried to buy some…" Adam stopped in the middle of the living-room. "What's wrong?"

He could see the look on Granny's face. He knew something was up.

"We need to talk, son." Granny patted the couch beside her, and Adam sat down, looking concerned.

"Is your leg hurting you?" he inquired.

"No dear. It's not my leg. Thanks for asking, though."

"What is it then?"

"Your daughter."

"Amirah?"

Granny just looked at him.

"What's wrong with Amirah?" He looked instantly concerned.

"You mean you haven't noticed how she's changed?"

Adam scratched his head for a minute and sat back on the couch thinking.

"Well, she's been a bit quiet lately, I guess. Especially since the earthquake," commented Adam.

"And, what else?"

"Yeah, she's quieter than usual, and a bit moody, but really Mum, I think it's all just a part of the process of her settling into a new country. She'll be all right once she starts school."

Adam was nodding his head as he spoke.

"Oh Adam. Sometimes you infuriate me!" said Granny, exasperated.

"What have I done?"

"Can't you see your daughter is growing up?"

"Of course! Anyone could see she's growing up. She's much taller now."

"Not just her height Adam! She's becoming a young woman now and I really think you're still treating her like a baby."

Granny looked toward the direction of Amirah's room and spoke in a loud whisper.

Adam looked down at the carpet, at the picture on the wall, at the plaster around the light on the ceiling – anywhere but at Granny's face.

"Well, that's the woman's department," said Adam quietly, half to himself. "I know she's moody, but I thought it was just her settling in," he added defensively.

"It's all happening to her at once," said Granny. "Moving to Egypt, all the traumas since we came, and her growing up and well, starting to spread her wings," remarked Granny.

"Her wings!" exclaimed Adam, looking serious. "What exactly do you mean?"

"I mean my dear son that the girl wants us to trust her more and feel like she's part of the adult world."

"Adult world!" exclaimed Adam. "This is serious," he thought.

Adam sat forward on the couch, running his hand through his beard, and moving from one side to the other. He was clearly uncomfortable with the subject.

"She's not going near the adult world!" said Adam with a fiery look. "Over my dead body!"

"Oh, for goodness sake Adam, the adult world is the real world. Where do you propose we keep her? In a cage somewhere? Shall we build her a cocoon?"

Adam stared blankly.

"Adam!" cried Granny.

Adam leaned back and closed his eyes. This was all happening too fast. It seemed like only yesterday when she was chopping up his sheepskin jacket and now…!

"I know it's difficult to see your little girl grow up," said Granny more gently. "And you've always done what's best for her all her life, haven't you?"

Adam nodded. He was looking down at the carpet, deep in thought.

"So why," continued Granny, "would you want to do things now that harm her?"

"I don't want to harm her. I'm not harming her! Of course, I don't want to harm her!" said Adam in a loud whisper. "But there are dangers out there that I can't protect her from!"

Adam stood up and pointed out the window with an intense glint in his eyes.

"Yes, you're right Adam," responded Granny, "but don't you think Amirah has to learn to tell the good from the bad herself. After all, you won't be around forever, dear."

"I won't?" Adam looked startled, almost feverish. Granny just looked at him.

"And neither will I son."

Adam started pacing around the room frantically. After a few minutes he went up to Granny, and said, "Okay. Where do I start then? Should I let her go to Roxy by herself? Or go downtown to do the banking.... It's just ridiculous! She'll be wanting to catch a bus by herself next."

Off he went again stomping up and down the living room.

"Two of a kind," muttered Granny, remembering Amirah's stomping act earlier that day.

"No Adam! She doesn't have to go to Roxy on her own, but she can go downstairs to buy some bread from time to time. There are lots of kids downstairs. They play and talk. Why on earth not? What's wrong with that?"

Granny was standing up now and she and Adam were face to face although Adam had to tilt his head downwards a bit to look into her eyes. He knew that look. It was the probably the first look he ever saw on his mother's face, and it meant 'now just be quiet and do as you're told.' There was no arguing with that look. And after all, he knew deep down that she was right, much as he hated to admit it. He had always known this day was coming, but did it have to come so soon?

"Okay," grunted Adam.

"Good," said Granny and she sat down on the couch again with a little smile on her face.

"Adam dear. We need some milk."

"Okay, I'll go now."

Granny rolled her eyes and stared at him.

"Not you," she whispered.

"Oh, oh, I get it. All right."

He walked the length of the living room again, took a deep breath, and then called out, "Amirah. Come here please."

CHAPTER 14

At Last!

Amirah walked into the living room.

"Yes, Dad. You wanted me?"

Adam swallowed a lump in his throat when he saw how sad and pale she looked. He gulped and coughed a little.

"Yeah, nip downstairs and get two pounds of bread for Granny and some milk. I got some of that *ful* and what's-its name and we're starving so run along. Hurry up then."

Adam was trying to sound relaxed. Amirah looked at Adam then at Granny then she raced out of the room and was back within two minutes.

"I'm ready," she chirped. "Anything else? Like fruit? Oh, and Dad there's an ATM just down a bit. Do you need any money?"

Adam looked like his eyes would pop right out of his head.

"That ATM is about three buildings down! I said to the supermarket downstairs – not halfway across town!"

"Oh Dad," said Amirah, putting on her sandals at the front door, "I can take care of myself. "
She patted him on the arm.

"Don't worry Dad. I'm a woman now."

Adam faced the wall and gently pounded his head against the cupboard. He sighed and tried to control himself. Still facing the wall, he said, "Don't talk to anyone, do you hear?"

Granny came over to give Amirah some money.

"How can she buy anything without talking Adam. She doesn't know sign language!"

Granny winked at Amirah. Amirah blew her a kiss. Adam continued to gently pound his head on the cupboard.

"Look, it's such a nice day Dad, I might go for a bit of a walk and buy the bread on the way back. Is that okay?"

Amirah wanted to see how far he'd go.

"Just to the shop and back and I'm timing you!" Adam was facing her now. Granny watched them. It was just like when Amirah chopped up his sheepskin jacket and they were playing tug-o-war with teddy. Granny started to smile, then to laugh. Both Amirah and Adam looked at her in surprise.

"What's so funny?" they both asked together.

"Honestly! Just go to the shop, would you?" said Granny.

"I'm off. See ya'. *Salam alaikum*."

Amirah closed the door behind her and skipped down the stairs with a broad smile.

Adam raced toward the front door. Granny stood in front of him.

"Adam let her go."

Adam ran to the balcony.

"I can't see her!" he called out to Granny.

"If you keep leaning over the balcony like that you might end up meeting her downstairs." Granny just shook her head.

"Really Mum, I can't see her."

"There are two shops downstairs. Perhaps she went to the other one."

Adam came back into the living room looking troubled.

"I never thought you would be such a worrier, dear."

Adam felt tired and sat down.

"Being a parent isn't easy," he reflected.

Granny laughed. "You're telling me!"

CHAPTER 15
City of the Dead

"What time is Shadiya coming to take us out today?" asked Adam.

"Any time now," replied Granny.

"But I thought she was just taking me out," exclaimed Amirah.

She didn't want to hurt her dad's feelings, but she was looking forward to spending some time on her own with her new friends, even if they were older than her.

"But I thought we were all going," stuttered Adam. He looked at Granny.

"No dear. Remember, we agreed it would just be Amirah. Sorry, perhaps there was a misunderstanding?" Granny looked at him.

"Amirah's a responsible young lady and she is in good company. *Insha Allah* there's nothing to worry about," Granny reassured Adam.

Adam looked at Amirah, who was waiting for them to arrive. They were already about half an hour late. She looked so grown up in that green scarf. He started to shake his head.

"Amirah! Do you know how to say our address in Arabic?"

Amirah rattled off the address very clearly.

"And the phone number?"

Again, she said the number perfectly as well as Adam's mobile phone.

"Shouldn't I take your mobile with me just in case?" asked Amirah, trying her luck.

"Just in case of what?" cried Adam anxiously.

"No need dear. You don't need your dad's mobile phone," said Granny, trying to change the subject. "You'll be just fine, *Insha Allah*."

The doorbell rang and Amirah dashed across the

room to open it.

"*Salam alaikum* Aunty Shadiya," said Amirah warmly.

The tall lady kissed Amirah four times, hugged her, and did the same to Granny. She nodded politely to Adam and introduced her daughter, Ranya. Granny brought in some juice, and they sat down to talk.

"Where are you off to today?" asked Adam, trying to sound like he wasn't interrogating anyone.

"We thought it would be nice to go to the Pyramids," said Ranya, looking at Amirah and smiling.

"The Pyramids!" said Adam, standing up.

"Very nice," said Granny before Adam could say anything else.

"I guess you've been there before?" said Adam, suddenly feeling rather awkward.

"Yes, many times but unfortunately today the car has broken down so we're going by bus. You don't mind, do you Amirah?"

Amirah looked surprised. She was looking forward to riding in Aunty's nice car but the thought of going out for the day meant she didn't care about taking a bus or two.

"No problem at all."

Granny smiled and winked at Amirah.

"We've ridden buses before, haven't we Granny?" said Amirah.

"Oh yes, many times," said Granny, nodding her head.

The ladies got up to leave.

"Are you ready then Amirah? We really should be going. We're going to a lovely little perfume shop called *Aida Perfumes*. It takes time to get there, and it will be quite crowded today."

"Will it?" asked Adam worriedly. "What time do you expect to be home?"

"Not sure really. What time do you like?"

"Any time at all," interrupted Granny. "Just have a lovely day, *Insha Allah*."

Before they left Adam grabbed Amirah and pulled her aside.

"Remember," he said in a whisper. "Don't talk to strangers, don't leave Aunty's side, don't go anywhere dangerous, and don't well, don't come home late and oh, have a good time. And I trust you. Okay?"

"Yeah Dad. I know you do." Amirah smiled and

gave her dad a kiss on the cheek.

"Don't worry so much Dad. I'll make the *du'aa* before I leave the house. And like I told you before I'm a woman now. I'll be just fine."

Adam hung his head in dismay.

"*Salam alaikum*, see ya'll later. Bye!" called out Amirah as she hurried down the stairs.

She was gone in an instant. Granny had to lead Adam back to the living room, sit him down and make him some tea.

※

Aunty Shadiya stood in front of the two girls and waved a bus down. It stopped. Amirah was surprised.

"There must be a knack to that too," she thought, remembering how many times Granny had waved buses down until one had stopped.

It was a normal hectic day in Cairo and the roads were filled with traffic. They had to stand up on the bus. After a few stops they got off and headed toward the main bus station.

"Keep close Amirah. It will be very crowded here, but I think you've ridden buses before, haven't you?"

asked Aunty Shadiya.

Aunty Shadiya was an old friend of Granny's. When Granny had come to Egypt throughout the years, she always visited Shadiya. It was Shadiya who had taught Granny to read Qur`an so many years before. She was a bit younger than Granny and was very tall and solidly built. Amirah felt safe with her. She seemed to be in control of all around her. Her daughter, Ranya, followed her like a shadow and didn't talk much.

"Have you been to many places in Cairo?" asked Ranya, as they stood up in the bus, holding tightly onto a pole.

"No, not really," said Amirah. "Not yet anyway. But I plan to!" she added.

"You'll have to see the Pyramids, the Citadel, the Museum, and the City of the Dead," noted Ranya.

"Don't be silly," said Aunty Shadiya. "There is nothing to see in the City of the Dead."

Amirah looked startled.

"What's the City of the Dead?" asked Amirah curiously.

"Nothing really, dear. It's just a huge area of graves where poor people live. We won't go there.

Honestly Ranya."

Ranya looked down and said no more.

They shuffled off the bus and the crowd closed in and the three of them had to push their way toward a large red bus. Aunty Shadiya was a bit in front and called out to Amirah, "It's the red bus, Amirah. That one."

Everywhere Amirah looked there were red buses, but she followed Aunty's direction and kept pushing.

"Come along," urged Ranya, who was hurrying to catch up with her mother.

There were now about three or four men between Aunty Shadiya and Ranya, and Amirah. Then Amirah dropped her bag. She quickly stooped to pick it up. Someone had already walked over it and when she bent down to scoop it up, a rather large woman carrying a crate of soft drinks on her head bumped into Amirah and sent her flying. The lady uttered words that Amirah interpreted to be an apology because of the look on her face, and the fact that she reached down and helped Amirah up and dusted off her clothes. Impressively, the lady did all that while balancing the crate of soft drinks on her head!

Amirah was amazed. When the lady saw that she

was all right, she left, heading off into the crowd. Now Amirah was standing up with her bag safely in her hands and she started looking around for Aunty. Two buses up she saw a large woman who looked just like Aunty, so Amirah headed up there. Just as she got there, the bus took off. So, Amirah ran and jumped on board. She'd seen it done often enough and was rather proud that she'd managed to do it.

The bus was packed like all the others, and Amirah had to maneuver her way to where some women were standing. She peaked through the passengers to where Aunty was standing at the front of the bus. The bus rocked and rattled out of the bus station and Amirah paid a man for the ticket and grabbed hold of the pole. The women on the bus smiled at her and Amirah waited for a break in the crowd so she could work her way up to where Aunty was. Finally, some people got off the bus and Amirah inched her way toward the bus driver. The bus was hurtling down the road now, in and out of traffic. She had to hold on to the back of the seats as she went. Then she came near to Aunty and tapped her on the shoulder. A strange face turned around and glared at her.

"But I thought you were Aunty!" said Amirah to herself.

Amirah frowned and looked around her on the bus. She could not see anyone who looked like Aunty and Ranya. How could she have been so foolish? Where did they get separated? Was it when she fell?

Amirah's heart was pounding. After a few minutes the bus turned a corner and went down a bumpy road and started weaving in and out of small brick buildings. They were single-floor structures. They didn't have windows and didn't look like houses.

"They look strange," she thought to herself.

Amirah realized that the most important thing she had to do now was to find out where she was. She looked around and saw a woman with a kind face, so Amirah asked her in her best Arabic, "Where are we now?"

To Amirah's surprise, the woman spoke English and answered her. "We are in the City of the Dead."

She said it so matter-of-factly and was so happy to be speaking to a foreigner that she didn't register the impact of her words. Amirah couldn't speak. What on earth would she do now?

Then a man came up to her. He had heard the conversation. He too spoke in English.

"You'd better get off here and walk back to the main road. It's not far and at the main road get a taxi. It's easy."

He nodded and smiled. He looked friendly. Before Amirah could say yes or no, the man had told the driver to stop, and Amirah found herself on a dusty road in the middle of the City of the Dead.

It was a sad sight to see that bus rattle off, rocking from side to side as it disappeared down the road. She was so bewildered that she hardly cared about the black smoke that filled the air from the exhaust. She couldn't really think at all.

CHAPTER 16

What Now?

Amirah stood on the side of the dirt road. She mustered up her courage and started to take in her surroundings. It was midday. Nothing to worry about. She tried to convince herself that everything was just fine. She remembered the name of the perfume shop they were planning to go to: it was *Aida Perfumes*. She would find it! She'd make her way to the Pyramids, and they'd meet up, *Insha Allah*. But try as she might, Amirah couldn't ignore the fact that she was alone in the middle of the City of the Dead.

In fact, it didn't really make any difference if she was alone or not, because all she could see was small streets lined with these little brick structures; 'graves', without a soul in sight. The streets were very clean and neatly swept. Shoes were placed neatly outside entrances. It all seemed unreal.

There was nothing else to do but start walking. She clutched her bag tightly and started making *du'aa*.

"Please Allah get me out of here safely and make me brave."

She felt afraid. She felt like a balloon that was ready to pop. Amirah felt that if she just let go of her self-control for one second, and let her racing thoughts take over, she would start running and screaming. She walked in carefully measured steps and kept praying, telling herself that everything was okay.

Each grave had an iron door. Many of them didn't have a roof but some had make-shift ones that had been added on. She remembered Ranya telling her that poor people lived here but she couldn't see anyone. Where were all the people? The wind started to blow and an electric light bulb hanging near the entrance of one of the small buildings swung from side to side. Something about it made her remember the earthquake and she shuddered.

The wind made strange sounds as it whisked in and around the graves and whipped Amirah's face. She kept her head high, straightened her shoulders and walked. After she had walked for some way and nothing happened, she started to relax a bit and think about her surroundings. Behind one of the graves, she saw a rope extended from a tree to a wall with washing hung out to dry. Then a bit further on she saw some books in plastic bags neatly arranged outside the entrance to one of the graves. There were signs of people living there but she had yet to see anyone. Were they sitting inside the graves, watching her?

She kept walking. She expected to hear footsteps behind her or a dog bark or someone laugh a wicked awful laugh somewhere in the distance, but there was nothing. Not a person. Nothing. A sense of eeriness crept over her. What if someone jumped out of the shadows and pulled her into one of the graves? Amirah frightened herself with these thoughts and tried to focus her mind on the perfume shop, the Pyramids, and her family. She started to walk more quickly.

Thoughts poured into her mind. She began to think what it would be like to live in such a place. She wondered how the people got to live there. Didn't they have any other place to go? Were there really children who were born and raised in a grave then went to school and got a job...? It seemed incredible. How would you tell someone where you lived? What would the other people think of those who lived in the graves? They must be thought of as the poorest of the poor because who would live in a grave if they had any other choice?

Amirah started to envision going to sleep at night in a grave. She really had to stop thinking about all this. She kept walking. She couldn't help but ponder on how poor the people must be. Where did they get their food from? She couldn't see any shops. Did the children go to school? Where were the people? That was the most amazing part of it all. Until now she hadn't seen anyone. Maybe there were no people here, after all. Maybe Ranya was just joking with her to make her afraid. Maybe. Then Amirah saw something that made her sure there were people who lived here.

She stopped in amazement. In fact, at first, she couldn't believe her eyes. She stood and looked at a billboard advertisement for soft drinks. An advertisement for soft drinks in the City of the Dead! The whole situation was becoming more and more unreal. The irony of it all! How could poor people living in such a place afford to buy soft drinks? Then when Amirah moved closer and looked at the advertisement, she saw it had been chained and bolted to the iron post. What are they afraid of? Are they afraid someone will try to steal it? Amirah shook her head in disbelief. Maybe the best use of that advertisement was to make a roof over one of the graves. Yeah, maybe that's why they chained it to the pole.

Amirah continued walking and thinking, and before she knew it, she had arrived at the main road.

"*Alhumdulillah*," she said out loud.

She heaved a sigh of relief. She had made it safely. Amazing. She had done it.

She flagged down a taxi. It stopped! She told the driver in her best Arabic, "The Pyramids, please." She felt confident but was still shaking inside. She was going to see this day through, *Insha Allah*.

CHAPTER 17
The Pyramids!

The taxi pulled up outside *Aida Perfumes*. It was a clean little street, at the end of which the Pyramids looked over a village. There were palm trees lining the road and their long, elegant branches swayed in the breeze. Amirah looked around and saw the pretty perfumes in the shop. She peered in the shop window. Someone immediately came out and was joined by another man who had been sitting on a chair near the door. Both men were wearing long, loose *jalabeyas* and one of them had a scarf tied around his head. They both had thick black moustaches and cheery smiles.

"Welcome! Welcome!" they said.

The older one introduced himself as Tarek and told Amirah that his family had had this shop for generations. You could tell he was very proud of it. Amirah was trying to take it all in. The exciting atmosphere of the place. The camels, donkeys and horses wandering down the street carrying tourists. She smiled and entered the perfume shop. The walls were lined with dainty glass shelves. Exquisite arabesque-style glass bottles containing essential oils were arrayed under special lighting along the walls of the shop. An assortment of beautiful smells filled the air. There was every type of perfume you could imagine. A comfortable arabesque bench hugged the walls. Amirah felt she had walked into an entirely different world. She was overcome by the sheer beauty of the place and forgot everything else.

"Are you here alone?" asked Tarek, looking concerned.

"Me? No! I'm meeting a friend of mine. Maybe she's been here?"

"What's her name?" he asked.

"Shadiya and her daughter is Ranya. We got separated at the bus station, but we were supposed to come here today."

"No," replied Tarek, shaking his head. "No one of that name came today and I'm sure if you got separated, she would be asking about you."

Ramadan, Tarek's brother, was standing behind them and he nodded his head. He spoke quietly to Tarek.

"What's your name?" he asked.

"My name's Amirah. Amirah Stevenson," she said with an air of confidence that surprised even herself.

"Okay Amirah. It's not safe for a young girl to be here at the Pyramids alone. There are many dangers in the world, you know."

Aminah had certainly heard *that* often enough.

"If you want to wait until your friend comes, you can wait here but don't go off on your own. Okay? We are your family."

Tarek patted his brother on the back and they both smiled warmly.

"Would you like some tea?"

Amirah nodded. Within minutes tea was brought out in the tiniest glass she'd ever seen. The tea was strong and sweet, and she felt the tension melt away. She sat there for some time and gazed out onto the street.

The camels trudged patiently along the sandy street, and donkeys and horses pulling wooden carriages took tourists from all over the world on a bumpy ride around the Pyramids. She was amazed at the huge camels lunging and swaying as they moved. One man was showing off on a camel, pretending he was a cowboy, but the camel simply leaned over a bit too far, and the man toppled off. Everyone laughed, except the man who dusted off his pants and disappeared into a shop. The tourists were followed around by young boys carrying small sticks to guide the massive animals. All the animals were tame and well-behaved. Tarek saw Amirah looking earnestly out of the window and asked her if she would like to see their animals.

"Do you have camels and horses too?"

Tarek laughed. "Oh course! Come with me."

Amirah got up and went out onto the pavement under the shade of the shop entrance.

"Sit here," said Tarek. He pointed to a cane chair with a comfortable cushion. He spoke to a young boy who smiled and brought a stunning-looking horse.

"This," said Tarek proudly, "is a dancing horse."

"Oh really? It dances?"

"Yes. Watch."

The boy got on the horse's back. There was no saddle, just a hand-woven multi-colored saddle cloth that looked rather prickly and uncomfortable. The reins were a simple bit of rope tied to the horse's harness. The boy talked to the horse and gave soft whistles. The horse pricked up its ears and started to move. Its strong muscles rippled, and its beautiful soft grey color shimmered in the sunlight. The boy pressed his heels onto the horse's left flank and the horse skipped and danced a bit to the right, then the left, then it arched its neck and bowed. But it didn't take long before it grew tired and started to buck, and the boy had to hold onto its mane to save himself from falling off. Tarek laughed. "More practice!" he called out, pointing to the boy.

Amirah laughed. Her eyes were lighting up with joy. "That was wonderful," she said.

Ramadan approached again and spoke to Tarek quietly and again Tarek smiled and nodded.

"Amirah. Do you want to see the Pyramids? I can let Ahmad take you around, and if your friend comes, I'll tell her to wait here for you. This is a present. No money."

Amirah didn't know what to say. The idea of going to the Pyramids was amazing and she was filled with excitement. Then she remembered her dad and Granny. She really should call them. Maybe they had found out that she and Aunty had got separated at the bus station. They would be worried! Amirah hadn't thought of them before. She'd been thinking that Aunty would find her at the Pyramids, but now quite a few hours had passed. Maybe she had gone home and told her dad. She'd better do something.

"Mr. Tarek can I use your phone?"

"Certainly."

He ushered her to the front desk just inside the doorway of the perfume shop and Ramadan dialed the number she gave him. It was busy. Amirah looked worried. Then she tried her dad's mobile number. It was busy too.

"Amirah. I can keep trying to call these numbers and when someone answers, I'll tell them you are here. So, you can go on your trip around the Pyramids. It will only take one hour or so."

Amirah thought about it. It made good sense.

"Okay," she answered pleasantly, though her stomach was now churning as she knew her family must be worried. But then she looked at Ramadan and she felt confident he would keep his promise. They were all so decent.

When she went outside the shop, Tarek asked her, "Do you want horse, donkey, or camel?"

Amirah had never had to make that decision before. She had ridden horses before with her friend in Australia, but camels and donkeys – never! "I think a horse will be fine, please."

Before she knew it, she was being helped up onto a solidly built brown horse.

"Is this a dancing horse?" asked Amirah.

"No! No dancing horses for tourists!" said Tarek.

"But I'm part of your family," reminded Amirah, jokingly.

Tarek laughed and they were off. Ahmad, who had ridden the dancing horse, was her guide and with a colorful stick guided his horse and Amirah's toward the largest Pyramid.

CHAPTER 18
Inside the Great Pyramid!

"You see the Sphinx's nose?" asked Ahmad, as they guided their horses casually along the streets.

Amirah nodded as she held onto the reins of her horse loosely.

"Napoleon shot it off with a cannon."

"Really?" asked Amirah. She sat up straight and took a closer look at the ancient monument. The nose was certainly missing!

She was in a continual state of wonderment as the horses picked their way around the Pyramids, over rocks and dangerously close to slippery slopes.

"You know Amirah, thousands of people died building the Pyramids and the Pharoah didn't allow anyone to live who knew the design of the inside. They were killed and buried here."

He pointed to a piece of empty land between two structures. It looked lonely and forgotten.

Ahmad was a young boy, about ten years old. He rode horses, donkeys, and camels confidently and was able to speak several languages because of his daily interaction with tourists. He had never gone to school and probably never would. He and Amirah had stopped their horses at the small valley that appeared so desolate and sad. It was filled with rocks and golden-colored sand. No one would ever have thought it was a grave, where people had been so unfairly killed. But then the whole place was a grave, a huge rocky mass of graves. Amirah shuddered.

"There are three pyramids," continued Ahmad, settling into his usual spiel for the tourists. "That biggest one over there was for the Pharoah, and those two smaller ones were built for the queen and her son. But there are many smaller tombs around. In fact, they are finding more all the time."

Amirah gazed around and saw little structures poking up out of the rocky sand.

"You want to see inside of one?"

"Can I?"

Amirah thought quickly. A grave. Should she venture in to see what it's like? Didn't Granny say something about not building on top of a grave? Anyway, these are old graves. Does that make any difference?

As if he realized what she was thinking, Ahmad said, "It's not really a grave, it's more like a temple. Most of the mummies have been removed and taken to the museum."

"Does that make it any better?" thought Amirah. Finally, curiosity got the best of her, and she nodded.
In the distance she could hear Arabic music blaring from some nearby coffee shop. It gave the whole place a surreal atmosphere; the ancient and the modern – not that many differences really. Just that the ancient people made money out of the poor and now the tables were

turned, and the poor were making money out of the ancient!

Ahmad and Amirah jumped off their horses and Ahmad led them to a nearby temple. There was a stout, rather frightening looking man standing at the entrance. He had a scowl on his face, but when he saw Amirah, a tourist, approaching, he smiled broadly and stood up and saluted her. Amirah greeted him but didn't smile. She felt nervous for some reason.

Ahmad spoke to the man, and they argued for a few minutes in Arabic, then the stout man was quiet, and Ahmad gestured for Amirah to follow him. Once inside the entrance there was a lot of light as a massive hole gaped above. There were strong white pillars with delicate designs standing erect, looking stable and permanent. Amirah wandered around examining the walls and the fine inscriptions. There were the usual pictures of ancient Egyptians sowing the fields and harvesting; but the writing and drawings was lop-sided and strange, not like in the drawings in the tourist shops.

The hairs on the back of her neck stood up and she felt extremely uncomfortable.

"I want to leave Ahmad," she demanded quietly.

"Just have a look over here first," said her new friend.

He wanted to show Amirah some drawings in the corner of the small temple, but Amirah kept checking behind her as if someone was staring at her.

"Really Ahmad I want to go. I don't feel good."

Ahmad laughed.

"Okay. Did you know there is something very special about this temple?" he asked with a cheeky smile, as they returned to their horses.

"What's that?" asked Amirah, mounting her horse, glad to be out of there.

"The mummies haven't been removed yet. Too old. Too broken up."

Wide eyed, Amirah stared at the place at the entrance where Ahmad was pointing. Sure enough, on either side of the entrance, were two stone rectangular shapes perfect to fit a mummy in.

Amirah's face fell.

"That must be why I felt so bad," she thought. "Let's get out of here," she said to Ahmad.

Without waiting for him to control the horses, Amirah set off toward the biggest Pyramid.

Ahmad caught up with her just as she reached it.

"You're getting good at riding in the desert," he told her.

"How long have you been working with Mr. Tarek?" asked Amirah.

"Since I can remember," answered Ahmad. "I'm ten now."

Amirah looked at him and wondered if Tarek was a relative or just a friend. She felt too shy to ask him personal questions.

"*Ammo* Tarek has been looking after me since I was this big."

Ahmad held his hands to show the size of a toddler.

"I was born in the City of the Dead and my uncle sent me to live with *Ammo* Tarek and work with him. He's a good man," said Ahmad proudly.

Amirah nodded. City of the Dead? So, it is real. People really do live there. She didn't want to ask Ahmad any more questions. She felt it was rude to pry.

There was a lot of hustle and bustle outside the entrance to the biggest pyramid. The entrance was simply one of the huge rocks loosened near the base.

"I wonder how long it took to find which rock was the entrance," thought Amirah.

As if he knew what she was thinking, Ahmad said, "Many people died trying to find the way into the Pyramid. Over one hundred years ago they started digging. Some people say there is a curse."

Amirah stood and stared at Ahmad, the Pyramid and the people.

The Pyramid was made of huge rocks, each one about the height of Amirah. She wondered how anyone could possibly have carried those rocks.

"Did they get the rocks from this area?" asked Amirah.

"No," replied Ahmad. "The rocks were brought from a place very far from here. They used clever ways to bring them, but many people died. The slaves did the work. Not enough food. Got beat a lot. They died."

Ahmad chewed on the end of the crop with one leg crossed over the saddle. He was perfectly at home on the back of a horse.

Amirah stared again at the Pyramids, wondering if it was worth all the effort and all the lives it had taken to build them. Someone must have thought so.

"Where are those people going?" asked Amirah.

"Into the big Pyramid," said Ahmad. "Do you want to go?"

Amirah looked at the people and at the size and grandeur of the Pyramid. Its stony cold hard look gave it an unforgiving appearance, daring anyone who wished to penetrate its depths. She wondered how many people from all over the world dreamed of entering this fearful place. Could she miss this chance?

The fact that she had seen and faced so many challenges in one day gave Amirah a sense of confidence and daring that she didn't usually have. She felt good, perhaps even a little over-confident.

"Yeah, I'll go in," said Amirah. "After all, basically it's just a bunch of rocks, isn't it?"

Ahmad kept chewing on the crop and let the horse step around at its ease.

He looked at her.

"You're brave for a girl."

"Thanks. I think," said Amirah.

She stared at him, wondering what the big deal about a girl being brave was. Everyone had to be brave, didn't they?

Amirah left her horse with Ahmad and headed off toward the crowds. She paid her money and stood in the queue. There were all kinds of people from all over the world waiting with her. Some were standing in small groups chatting in German, Japanese, Russian, and English. Amirah didn't feel alone; she didn't think about it. She was concentrating on what she wanted to do, and she wanted to see inside the Pyramid. It was just a spur of the moment thing and she felt she had to satisfy this sense of excitement and adventure.

The people lined up and started to enter the Pyramid. The entrance was low, and she had to duck down. Once inside, the tunnel was divided into two: on the right for going in and on the left for going out.

CHAPTER 19

A Sorry Surprise

The phone rang. Granny answered.

"*Wa alaikum salam.* Yes Shadiya. What? When? How long until you'll be here? *La hawla wa la quwatta illa billah.*"

With trembling hands Granny put the phone down. She felt faint.

"What's wrong Mum?" Adam was sitting on the couch talking to a friend on his mobile. He looked up when the phone rang. He got up when he saw the change in his mother's complexion. He rushed over to her and helped her sit down.

"What's wrong?" he repeated.

"They've lost Amirah."

"They've what?"

Adam froze. His heart skipped a beat. He couldn't think or feel or move for a few moments. When he regained his composure, he stared at Granny.

"When did this happen? How long ago?"

"Shadiya said they lost Amirah at the bus station, and they searched for her everywhere but couldn't find her. They're on their way here."

※

It was gloomy and cold inside the Pyramid. As Amirah walked between the other tourists, she held onto the rope railing on the left and her right hand sought guidance by touching the wall on her right. The wall was hard and cold. The stones felt flat but somehow were rough under her hand. She couldn't help but think about how many hands had chipped away at those rocks to make them so smooth and level. How many hands? How many people died to make this grave! It was too wickedly mocking to think about and try to comprehend the evil that people can do. What kind of people would do that? And why? Then again, why did she, Amirah Stevenson, want to visit that person's tomb, and to go inside the tomb! The mummy was gone. The treasure had been taken. Ahmad had told her it was empty inside, so why was she here? She kept walking. She kept following the person in front of her. She wondered why the others had decided to enter the Pyramid. Were they just curious? Was it just a part of their tourist package?

    She wasn't sure whether she was walking up or downhill. Her sense of direction seemed to disappear and all she could see ahead of her was gloomy darkness, broken here and there by shadowy lights high up on the walls. The air smelt heavy and musty. There was only enough light to make out the shapes of the tourists. She couldn't see any distinct features or expressions on their faces. Everyone was bent over. It was impossible to stand up straight in the tunnel. She noticed that the people moving toward the tomb were walking slowly, but the people on the exit side were rushing, almost running, and sometimes tripping. She wondered when they would reach their destination. She wondered what she would see. She wondered how she would feel.

At last, the doorbell rang, and Adam went quickly to open it. He felt like a piece of himself had fallen away. He felt empty.

"Come in," he said shakily.

"I'm so sorry," said Shadiya, crying. "We told her to stay close. When we couldn't see her, we searched the whole station, but she wasn't there. I didn't know where to start looking, so I came here so we could think together."

They sat in silence for a while in the living room.

"You were planning to go to the Pyramids, right?" said Granny, taking a deep breath. "Then she'll either come home or go there."

"Right," said Adam unevenly.

"So, if she hasn't come home then I think she will have gone to the Pyramids hoping to find you there," suggested Granny, feeling more hope that they would find her.

"Of course, no one would have taken her," said Shadiya, wiping her face nervously.

Adam stood up. His eyes looked angry and full of fear.

"No, *Insha Allah*, not," said Granny. "Amirah is very good at martial arts and if someone tried to do that she would yell and scream and would have a very good chance of fighting back. Sit down Adam and think with me," said Granny firmly. She could tell he was about to lose control.

"What is the name of the place you said you were going today?" asked Granny.

"*Aida Perfumes*," answered Shadiya.

"Then I think we should look there first," she said.

Just then the phone rang, and Adam rushed to answer it.

"A*ssalam alaikum*," said Adam. "Ramadan? Where? *Aida Perfume*s shop? When? What's the address? Thank you. Yes, we're coming right now."

Adam's face was bright. "She went to the shop! *Alhumdulillah*. What a blessing!"

Granny sighed with relief and Shadiya closed her eyes in gratitude. Adam had never in his life before felt such a huge feeling of relief.

Unexpectedly, Amirah found herself at another opening. This one was very low, and she had to bend down low to get inside. When she entered the room, she stared in wonder. This was it! The burial chamber. It was large with dark grey granite walls. The room was completely empty. People were standing in the middle of the chamber staring up at the ceiling, down at the stone floor and at each other.

One man said, "This place gives me the creeps. I'm out of here!"

He ran from the chamber.

"Me too," said another person.

Then one after the other the people moved back down the tunnel. Amirah felt very uneasy. She tried to imagine what the first discoverers had seen and felt when they found the chamber after so many years of searching. Then here she was, and it was empty but the feeling she had was so intense that she knew she didn't belong here. There was too much history, too many stories, too much heart break and disaster built into the walls, floors, and ceiling of this place. All she could think about was how to get out of there; as fast as she could. She shouldn't be there. She had no right to be there. This was a desecrated grave. She fled down the tunnel.

"Your face is all red," observed Ahmad when Amirah mounted her horse.

"I've never been so glad to get out of a place," she said with relief.

She basked in the sunshine and closed her eyes to feel the gentle breeze on her face.

"Imagine being locked in there," she thought. She shuddered. "Let's go," she said.

Their ride back to the shop was uneventful and Amirah's mind was whirling with the day's events.

"I'll have to call Dad and Granny when I get back to the shop," she told herself.

When the two riders rounded the corner and entered the street where the shop was, Amirah saw a tall figure with curly blonde hair. She looked again and sure enough there was the sheepskin jacket and comfy trainers.

"Dad!" she shouted. She jumped off the horse and ran over to him.

Adam didn't say a word. He hugged her and blinked back tears. Granny came over and stood beside them. She smiled warmly and took Amirah by the hand.

"Come on dear. Let's go and thank Mr. Tarek." Tarek was standing with Ramadan. They were both smiling broadly. Their shop was full of tourists and the bell on the front door didn't stop jingling.

CHAPTER 20
Another Memory

Granny, Adam, and Amirah sat in the back seat of a taxi, feeling relieved and happy.

"The calm after the storm," said Adam, gazing lovingly at Amirah.

"Don't say 'storm' Dad! You'll give me nightmares."

They all laughed remembering the windstorm, the taxi, the earthquake, and today.

"You've many things to write down in your diary," said Granny, giving Amirah a nudge.

"Oh yes, I'll do that tonight or maybe tomorrow, *Insha Allah*," said Amirah. "Dad, I don't want to go home right now. Can we go to the river?"

"Haven't you had enough adventure for one day?" he asked.

Amirah smiled. "That was when I was on my own. I want to go somewhere with you guys."

Granny nodded. "I think that's a nice idea. What do you think Adam?"

"No problem."

He leaned over and asked the taxi driver to take them to the Nile River.

"Can we go on one of those small boats?" asked Amirah.

Adam hesitated. It had been quite a day. But in the end, he said, "Sounds good."

As they drove along the highway, they saw a huge lorry that had stopped. The driver had spread his prayer mat in front of the parked truck. He prayed on the side of the road. Amirah smiled. He was a poor man. His clothes were old and ragged, but he still found things to be grateful for. This sight made her feel content and happy.

It also made her feel proud. She realized it was Islam that made her strong and brave enough to face difficulties. Just like it made this poor man pray.

The *faluka* floated silently down the Nile River and the small family sat quietly, enjoying the fact that they were together, and that Amirah was back safe and sound. As they gazed at their surroundings, they also felt grateful to be here in this country so filled with amazing wonders. The old man who steered the boat sat quietly near the rudder. He didn't talk. He seemed very calm. His life on the river had made him more at ease than the folks bustling around in the cars and buses on the busy streets.

Amirah was thinking about the many things she had seen that day.

"Poor people usually get the rotten end of the stick, don't they?" she observed.

"Unfortunately, that is often the way, Princess," said Adam quietly.

He looked at her closely. Granny was right. She had grown and changed since they first arrived in Egypt. Maybe the life here would make her grow up fast. He clasped her hand and squeezed it.

"I think we should do something to help the poor people," stated Amirah.

She couldn't stop thinking about the people who had built the Pyramids and those living in the City of the Dead as well as the poor people she saw all the time on the streets of Cairo.

"We do," said Granny.

"What do we do?" asked Amirah, puzzled.

"Every month we give money to an organization that helps them," said Adam.

"Why don't I do something as well? But I don't want to just give money. "I want to help people face to face," commented Amirah.

"You can," said Granny. "Anytime you like."

"But I want to do it with a plan. Would that organization let me help?"

"I'm sure they will *Insha Allah*," said Adam. "There's one not far from where we live. They have a *masjid* with a center next door that does vocational training, gives people a stipend every month, helps widows, orphans, and refugees."

"And," added Granny, "I heard they have counted the orphans living in a huge area of Nasr City and they give food and clothes to them every month. They're really organized in doing good."

"Well, I want to help them. I could go a few times a week. I could go there and help." Amirah was determined.

"That's a good idea," said Adam. "I'll phone and ask the person in charge."

"I can phone Dad. Just give me the number." Granny winked at Adam and nodded her head.

"Oh yeah, sure. I've got the number at home. I'll give it to you later," said Adam. "Listen Princess. I know you've been feeling bored and frustrated lately with being stuck at home and all that. But it won't be long before you start school and then you'll see, you'll make heaps of friends. It'll be great, *Insha Allah*," observed Adam.

Amirah stared into the depths of the Nile. School, new friends, the centre to help poor people – she felt that everything was finally starting to fit into place. Strange how things had changed since they'd first arrived.

"You know," she said quietly, "I think Egypt is going to be okay."

"Egypt? Or us?" smiled Adam.

"Well, Egypt is Egypt. I guess, I mean I'm going to be okay," said Amirah thoughtfully. "I've braved a windstorm, survived an earthquake, learned how to catch a taxi, and walked through the City of the Dead...."

"And been inside the biggest Pyramid!" added Granny.

"That was nothing," said Amirah with a smug look. "But you know I had to bow really low when I entered the main chamber."

"Yeah, the Pharaoh did that to make all the people bow when they entered. It was some kind of forced respect and humiliation," commented Adam.

"He was good at that," added Amirah. "If I'd known that, I would have gone into the chamber backwards!"

"I wouldn't have gone inside for all the tea in China!" said Granny.

"Really?" asked Amirah.

"You're joking! Go inside a grave! Never! A tomb! Spooky stuff, plus me being claustrophobic!" said

Granny, rolling her eyes. "Graves are for the dead – not the living. Believe me Amirah, you're much braver than me."

"But I'd never go inside it again," said Amirah. "Graves shouldn't be dug up and really, it's not a place for people to just go and see like they're visiting a mountain or some wildlife or something. It's like … it's a place where you should be afraid." They sat in silence for a while.

"What about you Dad? Am I braver than you?"

"That's a hard one," said Adam, nestling down in the seat and watching the little waves bump against the side of the boat. "I'm learning about myself all the time. I often wonder when I'll stop being such a … a… well, you know."

"Wimp?" suggested Amirah.

"Don't be cheeky!" He tweaked Amirah's nose. "I always thought I could brave any storm."

"But you couldn't cross the road, remember!" said Amirah.

"Well, I've learned since then, but…" he continued, "I never felt as afraid as I did today when I thought I'd lost you."

"So, you've faced your greatest fear. Good for you son," said Granny, looking lovingly at Adam.

"And I didn't use to be afraid of anything until that plane incident in Bangkok. Remember Granny?" commented Amirah.

"How could I forget?"

"I guess I'm a survivor," added Amirah.

"Looks like," said Adam, "but I hope we don't have any more catastrophes for a long, long time."

Amirah gazed again at the water. She would open her mum's patchwork box again when she got home. She couldn't see into the future. "Only Allah knows that," she thought. "My life is something like these waters," she pondered. "It's like layer after layer of things happening to you and then learning, and then more experiences and when you put it together in the end, it's your life."

She had no way of knowing what she would face in her life, but at that moment, she decided to face whatever comes, with courage.

Glossary

1. *Allah*: Arabic for God.

2. *Alhumdulillah*: All praise and thanks be to Allah.

3. *Ammo:* uncle (often used when speaking to an older male even if he is not a relative, out of respect).

4. *As salam alaikum*: Islamic greeting meaning 'peace be with you'.

5. At the drop of a hat: very quickly

6. *A`udhubillahi mina ash-shaitanar-Rajeem*: I seek refuge with Allah from the accursed Satan.

7. *Bismillah:* In the name of Allah

8. Bit of a dip: Go for a swim.

9. Bonkers: To go out of one's mind. A playful term.

10. Chuck me in: To throw me in.

11. Coyotes: A kind of wild dog that is also a character in the cartoon with the 'road runner'. The coyote is a foolish, greedy character that continually tries to catch the road runner but always fails.

12. *Du`aa*: Supplication to Allah, the Almighty.

13. Dumb: Foolish.

14. *Emirate al Oboor:* Oboor buildings. *Min Fadlak:* Please.

15. *Falukha:* Small sailing boat on the Nile River for people to hire and relax on.

16. *Fajr prayer:* Early morning prayer. One of the five compulsory prayers in Islam.

17. Forty winks: a nap

18. Freelance: To do contract work for different companies or selling one's work to them.

19. *Hadith*: Sayings and traditions of Prophet Muhammad (peace be upon him).

20. *Hijab:* A head covering worn in public by Muslim women. It also refers to general modesty of dress.

21. *Inshaa Allah*: If God wills.

22. *Istikharah*: A two *rak`ah* prayer followed by the *du`aa Istikharah* which is performed seeking Allah's guidance when making a decision.

23. *Jalabeyas:* A traditional Arab garment worn over clothing that is worn by men.

24. *Jazaka Allahu khairan*: 'May Allah bless you.' It is said by someone who is given something, as an alternative to saying thank you.

Amirah Stevenson Series

Book One

Buried Treasure

Twelve-year-old Amirah has a lot on her mind. She is being teased at school and lately had to confront a bully. She can't seem to connect with her dad and growing up without her mum just makes everything seem worse. How will she handle this? Who can she turn to?

www.ingramcontent.com/pod-product-compliance
Lightning Source LLC
LaVergne TN
LVHW041222080426
835508LV00011B/1041